'Tim has done a great job of [...]
helpful practical application, s[...]
effective spiritual leadership. I love this book [...]
to anyone in any sort of church/ministry leadership.'
James Aladiran, founder, Prayer Storm

'*Leadership 101* is written straight from the trenches of youth work and
is a gift to everyone involved in serving and loving young people in
any capacity! Tim lives and breathes this stuff and each chapter will
challenge, inspire and resource you to grow and develop as a leader
to best serve the next generation. Tim does a brilliant job of humbly
offering practical advice gained through many years of experience, as
well as leaving space for God to speak to you. This is a must-read, either
on your own or with some friends. So grab a journal and take it slowly,
because, to quote Tim, "I simply cannot conceive of anything more
necessary that you could give your life to than passing on the gospel to
the next generation."'
Susie Aldridge, Lead Pastor, Dreaming the Impossible, and Associate
Pastor, Trent Vineyard

'Tim is an outstanding leader and person. He models what he teaches
and carries such an authority in the youth ministry community with
humility and grace. This excellent book is packed full of practical,
lived-out wisdom. I love that this book is written by a youth ministry
practitioner for people working on the frontline. Like the best books,
this is not meant to be read alone but in community, so read it with
others, apply the wisdom in its pages and let's see our youth ministries
fly and flourish!'
Pete Baker, National Director, Pais Movement

'Tim is the real deal – an outstanding kingdom leader with a huge depth
of insight. I've learned so much from journeying with him and I've no
doubt you will too as you read through this book that's crammed with
practical wisdom.'
Carl Beech, founder, Christian Vision for Men and The Edge Network

'Practical, accessible, engaging and packed full of wisdom. This book
is an absolute must-read for anyone in youth and children's ministry.'
Gavin Calver, CEO, Evangelical Alliance

'More than a manual and way beyond a "how to" guide, this is a passionate, compelling invitation to the adventure of discovering and developing your life as a leader of children and young people. Hugely practical, *Leadership 101* is filled with insight and inspiration, resource and revelation. Tim is convinced that God is about to move afresh among generations of children and young people and that this is the greatest possible thing we could be involved in. Get this into the hands of every youth and children's leader you can.'
Chris Cartwright, General Superintendent, Elim Pentecostal Church

'Leadership isn't in your genes, it grows from your inner life. Tim takes us on a journey into how that happens with great insights and practical lessons. You'll want this book in your pocket, not on the shelf.'
Chris Curtis, Chief Executive, Youthscape

'*Leadership 101* is a fantastic resource enabling youth and children's ministers to reflect and grow in their leadership. Tim has written an incredibly practical book that offers huge amounts of simple but actionable advice that will see your leadership develop and grow. Tim is not afraid to move beyond established leadership models, tackling current issues such as social media and mental health and their impact on leadership. The book is a well thought-through and challenging manual of leadership from start to finish and comes thoroughly recommended.'
Jimmy Dale, National Youth Evangelism Officer, The Church of England

'This is a brilliant resource for youth and children's leaders. This book provides excellent wisdom, advice and practical steps to leading well with space for reflection and application throughout. I'd highly recommend it to anyone involved in ministry to children and young people as an easy-to-read but challenging and accessible resource.'
Paul Friend, Director, South West Youth Ministries

'There are books on leadership you know you're supposed to read, and then there are books on leadership that you must read. This is one such book. It's loaded with sharp wisdom and enduring encouragement fresh from the trenches of what it actually means to pastor and lead

young people. But what I appreciate most about this book is that Tim so evidently loves youth leaders and knows the unique challenges we face. Passionate, provocative and profoundly actionable, this book is a gift for everyone who shares God's heart for the emerging generations to know Life in all its fullness.'
Rachel Gardner, Director of Partnerships, Youthscape

'This book is not only really accessible, relatable and inspiring but also excellent both for those of us starting out on our leadership journey, and for those a little further along! I would however offer this warning: don't read this book too quickly as there is gold in here that you cannot afford to miss.'
Laura Hancock, Director of National Ministries, British Youth for Christ

'Tim repeatedly reminds us that there is no greater privilege than being called to serve children and young people. This is evident throughout the book with Tim's obvious love for young people, youth leaders and most importantly Jesus! This extremely readable and practical book is full of insight, wisdom and leadership gold, developed from years of being on the front line and wrestling with both the "why" and the "how" of what we do. The simple and profound nuggets of wisdom throughout this book will help you to lead yourself and the youth and children's ministry in a much more effective and fruitful way. Read it prayerfully, wrestle with the questions and let it really shape how you serve and lead!'
Andy Harding, Executive Pastor, Central Church, Director, PowerPoint, Vice Chair, Magnitude, and founder, Lead

'Tim Alford has learned these lessons not in the classroom but in the hurly-burly, heartbreaking, inspiring world of Christian leadership. It's required reading for every leader who wants to leave a legacy of fired-up leaders who totally follow Jesus. Is there really anything more important than that?'
Andy Hawthorne OBE, Director, The Message Trust

'We desperately need great leaders to navigate the extraordinary times we are living in. *Leadership 101* is the book the youth-ministry world has been crying out for to help develop Godly, skilful leaders full of

integrity and passion. Tim is the real deal and his punchy style, winsome storytelling and practical advice make this book accessible for leaders at every age and stage. It is a gift to the Church and I wholeheartedly commend it.'
Phil Knox, Head of Mission to Young Adults, Evangelical Alliance

'This book offers timely insight and real practical wisdom for any leader in any context. Whether you are strengthening your own leadership muscles, building an effective team or launching out into a new leadership landscape, this book offers you tools and suggestions that will get you off on the right footing.'
Dave Newton, Principal, Regents Theological College

'Tim writes really well! It is inspiring, encouraging and practical, helping those starting out in ministry, as well as the more seasoned, unpack and wrestle with the principles of leadership in our current times.'
Neil O'Boyle, National Director, British Youth for Christ

'A comprehensive guide to pretty well every facet of leadership written at an accessible level for those keen to tackle the challenge of reaching children and young people with the love of God. Read it prayerfully and I feel sure your work will change for the better.'
Andy Peck, Editor at Large, Premier Youth and Children's Work Magazine

'*Leadership 101* is a book I wish had been written when I was starting out. It is packed full of practical wisdom and insight. So, so helpful. A must-read for anyone involved in youth and children's ministry, but also a great resource for anyone who aspires to be an effective leader.'
Mike Pilavachi, Soul Survivor Watford

'I wish this book existed when I first started leading people! I think people wonder about the authenticity in books like this: "Is it just some guy with a bunch of nice leadership ideas?" Well, this book is nothing of the sort. Tim lives this stuff. And when I say "live", I mean he leads with excellence in local and national contexts and is committed to growing in every area of leadership himself.'
Dan Randall, Youth Director, HOPE Together

'Tim is passionate about developing good, Godly leaders who will last the course, and he has poured that passion into *Leadership 101*. This accessible, practical and wise book will help you to think and pray through every aspect of your leadership, and shape you into the kind of leader that children and young people deserve.'
Martin Saunders, Deputy CEO, Youthscape

'My first encounter with Tim was when he was leading worship at one of our national youth events. What I noticed at that time, and have continued to notice, is that Tim lives out and practises what he speaks about. Tim's first book, *Leadership 101*, is no exception to that. As I have read through these pages, I see a leader who has tried to live out what he has written. Leadership for Tim isn't just some abstract theory, it's a lived reality. This book will not only be a great inspiration to children and youth leaders but will also be a practical guide for their leadership in the local context. The impact of this book will not only make a difference in the lives of the leaders but also in the lives of the young people – calling on a generation to also be the leaders that God has called them to be.'
Helen Schofield, Territorial Youth and Children's Secretary, Salvation Army UK

'This book should be an essential part of a youth leader's toolkit. Work through it or dip into it! Either way, it will help you, inspire you, encourage you, stretch you and equip you for impactful, influential ministry with young people and your team. Tim writes with honesty and humour, drawing together biblical and leadership wisdom from the ages. Devour it and do it!'
Matt Summerfield, Zeo Church

'This book is like sitting over coffee with a friend and chatting about youth and children's work. It is funny, gentle, kind, challenging and full of wisdom. I couldn't put it down! It has become a permanent feature on my desk so that I can dip back in for more ideas and inspiration. Tim carefully guides us through understanding youth culture, church, leadership, strategy and, most importantly, the prioritization of young people. This is an important book for youth and children's work in our time.'
Dot Tyler, Head of Youth and Emerging Generation Team, Tearfund

'*Leadership 101* is a fantastic book that speaks into the here and now but also to the longevity of youth and children's ministry. It utilizes a wide range of perspectives and influences that help to frame a larger understanding of healthy ministry. This book is timely and a great resource for the young or seasoned children's or youth pastor to be constantly reminded of and given tools for mastering the basics.'
Dan Watson, Hillsong Youth UK

'There is no higher priority in our nation at the moment than to reach the emerging generation with the good news of Jesus. To achieve that, we need fresh leaders full of passion who will be committed to that cause. Tim Alford has spent his life in pursuit of that vision and now we have this book, full of his experience and wisdom, to inspire us all to more. There's no time to waste: get reading and let's mobilize leaders to kick-start a post-COVID world with the age-old call to follow Jesus.'
Pete Wynter, Leadership Pastor, Holy Trinity Brompton, and Director, Leadership College London

Tim lives in Malvern, England, with his wife Jen and two children, Tobijah and Aria. He is National Director of Limitless, Youth Ministry Specialist Lecturer at Regents Theological College and a volunteer youth leader. Tim is passionate about equipping leaders and communicating the gospel, having spoken at conferences, churches, schools and events all over the world. He is an enthusiastic – if average – runner, a frustrated supporter of Arsenal, and has on more than one occasion been to the cinema in Star Wars fancy dress.

LEADERSHIP 101

Your go-to guide for leading youth and children's ministries into a brighter future

Tim Alford

First published in Great Britain in 2021

Society for Promoting Christian Knowledge
36 Causton Street
London SW1P 4ST
www.spck.org.uk

British Library Cataloguing-in-Publication Data
A catalogue record for this book is available from the British Library

ISBN 978–0–281–08607–8
eBook ISBN 978–0–281–08608–5

Typeset by Falcon Oast Graphic Art Ltd
First printed in Great Britain by Jellyfish Print Solutions
Subsequently digitally printed in Great Britain

eBook by Falcon Oast Graphic Art Ltd

Produced on paper from sustainable forests

CONTENTS

Contents

Part 3

VISION AND STRATEGY

EVERYTHING RISES AND FALLS ON LEADERSHIP.

JOHN C. MAXWELL[1]

PREFACE
RISE AND FALL

———

Sounds like one of those pithy quotes that conference speakers use to ensure their audience takes to Twitter, right? But here's the thing, John Maxwell was right. Everything rises and falls on leadership.

Over the years of serving God in various forms of ministry I've been fortunate enough to visit more churches, para-church organizations, ministries and events than I'd dare to count. And in all those experiences I've noticed a trend that has been entirely without exception: *there is a direct correlation between the fruitfulness of a ministry and the quality of its leadership.* Always.

There are other things that have an impact on the fruitfulness of a ministry of course: resources, geography, demographic, training, style, approach, circumstances (both present and historic) all contribute, for better or worse. But when it comes to fruitfulness, none of these has nearly the impact of leadership. In every nation, and in every type of ministry, leadership is *the* defining factor that supersedes all other challenges and opportunities. Everything rises and falls on leadership.

Which brings us to this book. It's unlikely that you signed up for youth or children's ministry because you wanted to lead. You got into this because you had a passion to see children and young people encountering Jesus, and, as it turned out, leadership came as part of the package! And yet your capacity to see the things you long for realized will largely depend on your capability to lead.

This book, then, is designed to equip you with the tools you need to lead at your best; to lead your children and young people towards Jesus; to lead the best kingdom teams possible; to lead your youth and children's ministries into a brighter, more fruitful future.

There are two ways you can engage with this book. The first way is to read it like, y'know, a book! Start at the beginning and read it right through to the end for a broad spectrum of the skills, processes and characteristics you need to lead.

But that's not where the journey ends. This book has been written in short, quick-fire chapters in order to serve as something of a field guide as you continue on your leadership journey; something you can easily dip in and out of along the way. For example, you've got an important meeting with your senior leader coming up? Prepare yourself by revisiting 'How to lead up'. There's a difficult conversation you need to have with a team member? Take a few minutes to reread 'Shoot the elephant'. Or perhaps you've identified a leadership gift in one of your young people. Spend a moment reflecting on 'Pay it forward: raising leaders', to help you form a strategy for their development. You get the idea.

And that's why *Leadership 101* is created to be practical and actionable. Not just for information, but application. Each chapter comes with some questions for reflection, some of which are best processed on your own, and others together with your team. There's also a *Leadership 101* YouTube series to accompany the book, covering some of the same content but in a visual format.

However you use it, I pray that our time together will help you grow as a leader and more effectively reach and disciple young people as a result. So let's get going, let's get better, because everything rises and falls on leadership.

PART 1
SELF-LEADERSHIP

IT IS BETTER TO WIN CONTROL OVER YOURSELF THAN OVER WHOLE CITIES.

PROVERBS 16.32

INTRODUCTION
SHARPEN THE SAW

In his seminal work *The Seven Habits of Highly Effective People*, Stephen Covey asks us to consider the effort required to cut down a tree. It's a big task, exacting a great deal of effort and probably a lot of time . . . very much like youth and children's ministry!

So we take to the tree with our saw and begin to cut to and fro, back and forth. Progress is slow but definite; if we just keep going we will reach our target in the end. The job feels so big that we hate to take time away from applying ourselves to the task, and yet we know, in the long run, stepping away from the work in order to sharpen the saw will ultimately increase effectiveness, enabling us to reach our goal.

This is the principle of self-leadership. We take time away from the work in order to focus on our personal growth and development, knowing that (although it's hard to come away from the coalface) our ministry will ultimately be more effective as a result. Or, as Covey would have it, 'Private victories precede public victories. You can't invert that process any more than you can harvest a crop before you plant it.'[1]

Simply put, we cannot lead others until we first lead ourselves.

Before we think about culture and team building, or vision and strategy, we're first going to take a long, hard look at ourselves! What are the things we need to put in place in our own lives in order to ensure our vision stays fresh, our passion stays hot and our leadership stays effective? Let's sharpen the saw.

THE SINGLE MOST IMPORTANT THING YOU WILL DO TODAY IS TO SPEND SOME TIME WITH JESUS. CONSISTENTLY DOING THIS ONE THING WILL TOTALLY TRANSFORM YOUR LIFE AND MINISTRY.

01

THE TEN MOST IMPORTANT THINGS A LEADER SHOULD DO EVERY WEEK

For nine years I was part of a band. Our rehearsals were largely made up of disagreements, frustration and trips to Asda to get away from it all. But every now and then, out of the chaos would emerge something magical; a moment where everyone was personally, and musically, 'in the pocket'. A sweet spot where instrumentally and vocally everything was soaring. It felt good, it sounded great. We had found our rhythm.

We've all experienced moments like these in our life and ministry. There have been times where life seems to be spiralling out of control: pastoral issues, dysfunctional teams, sessions to plan, talks to write, disengaged young people, and strained relationships. It's hard, it's frustrating, we're exhausted, and Asda is our only escape! But every now and then we hit that sweet spot. We're on top of our workload, our team is united, our young people are passionate, our sessions are fresh, our relationships are deep and our work makes us feel alive. We've found our rhythm.

That's the place we want to live, right? So if you're there right now, how do you stay there? If you're not, how do you get there? I want to suggest the ten most important things leaders should do every week in order to find, and keep, their rhythm.

1 Devote

You knew I was going to say this, but this is number one for a reason. The single most important thing you will do today is to spend some time with Jesus. And the same goes for tomorrow. When we regularly stop to pray and open our Bibles (and not just to prepare our next session!), we open ourselves up to the renewing work of the Holy Spirit in our lives. We are stronger in our battles against sin, fresher in our revelation and more sensitive to the leadings of the Spirit. Our faith seems deeper, our resolve stronger, our courage greater, our vision clearer and our passion more contagious.

I agree wholeheartedly with Henri Nouwen when he writes, 'We do not take the spiritual life seriously if we do not set aside some time to be with God and listen to him.'[1] I am in no doubt that the best thing you could do as a result of reading this book is to prioritize spending time with Jesus every day. I promise you that doing this one thing will totally transform your life and ministry.

2 Reflect

To paraphrase pastor and leadership expert Andy Stanley, 'Experience doesn't make you better, evaluated experience does.' Which is why I've tried to build into my weekly rhythm a space to pause, reflect and innovate. The problem is that time for reflection has a way of surrendering to the tyranny of the urgent, quickly descending to the bottom of our to-do list. But we must resist this pull by planning, prioritizing and protecting time in our week for reflection.

When the coronavirus pandemic hit in the spring of 2020 and the UK went into lockdown, the first two weeks were a time of fast-paced response and adaptation. That was OK in the short-term, but I resolved early on not to allow that pattern to become a new normal. This was a time for *more* reflection, not less. So I duly scheduled extra time in my calendar for the important work of reflecting on the season and listening to God. And I'm glad I did. Out of that time came some truly radical ideas that I would have had no hope of discovering had I allowed this time for reflection to be swallowed up by the busyness carnivore. In fact, working the discipline of reflection into our rhythm is so important that we will dedicate the whole of the next chapter to exploring it further.

3 Read

Every great leader I know reads – a lot. The fact that you're reading this book tells me that you understand the value of this practice, even if it doesn't come naturally to you. Nice one! But once again, it's so easy for reading to get pushed to the bottom of our priority list for something more urgent. If you find this happens to you (as it does to me), then start off by maximizing your downtime. Read while you're waiting for the bus; read while you're sitting on the toilet (sorry!); read instead of scrolling through Instagram; read instead of watching Netflix. There is such a wealth of wisdom out there, so soak it up. Read leadership books, devotional books, theology books and youth or children's ministry books. And if you don't know where to start, the books listed in the notes at the back should keep you going for a while.

It's worth noting that if the written word is a particular challenge for you, there are other ways to take in the content, such as audio books and podcasts – so there's really no reason to circumvent investing in your leadership in this way.

7

So, leader, read all you can. Because reading doesn't only equip us with skills, it sets ideas and dreams percolating in our minds as we are inspired by the lives and leadership of others.

4 Collaborate

Are you a lone-ranger or a collaborator? Because leadership is not about ticking items off a to-do list; it's about inspiring a community of people to journey together towards a shared objective. There is no greater joy than seeing others grow because you gave them the opportunity, encouragement and support to do so. But this isn't a one-way street. Collaborating with others will push you to think of things you would never have considered on your own. As leadership consultant Brad Lomenick points out:

> Collaboration is integral for leaders moving forward. It is part of the framework for trading equity and value in today's economy. Collaboration is now the norm, not the exception. A catalyst leader wants to work together with all kinds of leaders and organizations, without worrying who gets the credit.[2]

The triune God models leadership in collaboration, and we'd do well to imitate him.

5 Encourage

One of the most important things leaders can do is to ensure they are not the centre of their own worlds. So humble yourself by elevating others. Champion your colleagues, your team and your young people. Don't let something they've done go by unrecognized or uncelebrated. Sing their praises privately and publicly. Be a cheerleader for others and watch their loyalty, work ethic, enthusiasm and determination skyrocket as you do. Becoming a person of encouragement is such an integral part of leadership that we will return to it in different contexts on several occasions throughout this book.

6 Serve

For a number of years I served at a fantastic church where our senior pastor would regularly encourage us to 'do something every day that reminds you you're a servant'.[3] Leadership is not about being at the top of the tree, it's about being at the bottom. The topsy-turvy, upside-down, radical kingdom leadership of Jesus demonstrates this in the most profound way: 'The greatest among you will be your servant,' he said (Matthew 23.11). The greater the leadership responsibility, the greater the requirement to serve. If you have been elevated by title or position, choose to lower yourself. Leverage whatever influence has been entrusted to you to champion the people around you.

7 Risk

Let me ask you a few provocative questions. How much faith does it require for you to live this week? What faith adventures are you on right now? In what way is your youth or children's ministry causing you to get on your knees and pray for God to show up? If it's not, perhaps it's time for you to dream a little bigger and take some audacious, God-sized risks – because you cannot grow in your comfort zone! The best place for leaders to live is just over the border of their capacity, ensuring we are not relying on our own gifts and experience, but rather in total dependency on God.

8 Work

All leaders who make a difference have this in common. They work. *Hard.* The mission is too important for anything less. Leaders who want to make a difference must aspire to show up and bring the very best of their energy and effort to God every day. These leaders have an allergic reaction to laziness. They squeeze the juice out of life. They maximize their time. They are faithful stewards of the responsibilities and opportunities that God has entrusted to them, taking that which he has given them and returning it to him with interest. So what does it mean for you to bring your 'first fruits' to God at work this week?

9 Exercise

What does exercise have to do with our leadership? Well, imagine having an extra 1.4 days a week to get everything done. It would be a game-changer, right? Did you know that proper exercise and rest patterns give us a 20 per cent energy increase in an average day, average week, average month? A simple weekly exercise routine could radically increase your capacity, energy and focus, and will certainly improve your mental and emotional well-being. So, what does exercise have to do with our leadership? Author Jo Saxton nails it: 'You have one body, and your leadership lives in it.'[4]

We make a mistake when we separate our physical health from our spiritual health. What we do with our bodies impacts our souls and we cannot separate the two. Finding a healthy rhythm of exercise will make a huge contribution to finding a healthy rhythm of life.

10 Rest

I'm willing to wager that if you stole something, killed someone or slept with someone other than your spouse, you'd feel pretty bad about it. So why is it that we almost feel proud of ourselves when we work seven days straight? 'Remember the Sabbath day' is not one of 'the ten suggestions'. As Rob Bell so beautifully puts it, 'Sabbath is taking a day a week to remind myself that I did not make the world and that it will continue to exist without my efforts.'⁵ So, stop thinking that you're way too busy and important to rest for 24 hours. Stop thinking this one is for everyone else except you. Stop working and do something that refills, refreshes and replenishes you. There can be no healthy rhythm without rest.

Application questions

- Are any of the ten areas outlined above absent from your weekly rhythms? If so, what might you need to stop in order to create space for these practices?
- Draw four boxes entitled, 'Spiritual disciplines', 'Relationships', 'Work' and 'Rest'. These 'boxes' may of course overlap in practice but are helpful for our purposes here. Take some time to reflect on the life-giving rhythms you want to prioritize in each of these areas, and write them in the boxes.

WITHOUT TIME TO PAUSE, REFLECT AND INNOVATE, WE CEASE TO GET BETTER AND OUR MINISTRIES PLATEAU. AFTER ALL, IF WE DO WHAT WE'VE ALWAYS DONE, WE'LL GET WHAT WE'VE ALWAYS GOT.

02
PAUSE, REFLECT, INNOVATE, REPEAT

___

When was the last time you took some pre-planned, extended time to stop and think? How often do you pause to take a 'big-picture' view of your youth or children's ministry? Where are the spaces and places you go to reflect on your practice and consider how you could innovate to make it better? And how regularly do you take time out of your usual routine to create space for God to speak to you? If your answer is 'not often', you could be in the danger zone.

Danger 1: Spiritual deficit

When you don't have enough time with God to sustain your doing for God, you begin to operate out of a spiritual deficit – giving out more than you are taking in – resulting in a loss of joy, diminishing passion, and a lack of ideas. This leads to stress, frustration, cynicism, apathy and, in extreme cases, burnout. As Peter Scazzero so powerfully reminds us,

> who you are is more important than what you do. Why? Because the love of Jesus in you is the greatest gift you have to give to others . . . Your being with God (or lack of being with God) will trump, eventually, your *doing* for God, every time. We cannot give what we do not possess. We cannot help but give what we do possess.[1]

So, do you have enough being with God to sustain your doing for God, or are you leading out of a spiritual deficit?

Danger 2: Lack of revelation

If you are not taking time to pause and reflect, you are robbing the people you lead of the thing they need from you most – revelation from Jesus. You are 'the blind leading the blind' and you will inevitably end up in a pit (Luke 6.39). God rarely speaks in the busyness, he speaks in the stillness; not in the noise, but in the whisper (1 Kings 19.11–13). So consider, are you in danger of making plans *for* God without actually listening *to* God? Because there is no shortcut to hearing from God that bypasses time in his presence.

Danger 3: Busy not fruitful

We end up filling our time with *good* ideas, and missing out on *God* ideas. In other words, we become busy but not fruitful – and make no mistake, busyness and fruitfulness are not the same thing. Busyness comes from multiplying activity; fruitfulness comes from being connected to the vine (John 15.1–17).

Danger 4: Plateau

We carry on doing what we've always done, just because we've always done it. But what if how we've always done it is no longer the best way to do it? Without time to pause, reflect and innovate, we cease to get better and our ministries plateau. After all, if we do what we've always done, we'll get what we've always got!

*

As you can see, the dangers associated with failing to prioritize time to pause, reflect and innovate are significant. And yet, due to the tyranny of the urgent, we are so quick to forsake these times. Pausing is later. Reflecting is later. Innovating is later. Urgent is *now*! So protecting these vital moments requires some forward planning, a lot of intentionality and a good deal of courage.

In the last chapter, we thought about creating a healthy weekly rhythm to sustain and develop our leadership. Now let's take this a step further by developing an annual, monthly, weekly and daily rhythm. What follows is an insight into the pattern that has helped me to stay out of the danger zone. The point is not necessarily for you to imitate this wholesale (though please feel free to take as much as you want!), but rather to use these ideas as a launch pad for creating your own regular time to pause, reflect and innovate.

Annually

At the start of each year I take two full days away from the regular routines, locations and, most importantly, technologies of life. This is a time to shut down my email account, disengage from social media and make extended time to pray, walk, study, think, dream and plan. I have found this an invaluable practice that sets me up for the year to come. It enables me to attack the year with a renewed energy and fresh ideas.

I remember one occasion in particular when God spoke to me in a way that refocused my whole year, and every year following. The Lord spoke to me about the three things he has put in me that add the most value to the ministry I serve: vision and strategy, leadership development, and public communication. He instructed me to devote 80 per cent of my working time to these three things. So, upon returning from this annual retreat, I began to attribute to these three things specific colours in my calendar so they would stand out from the other activities I attended to, ensuring that a quick glance at my weekly schedule would enable me to see clearly if I was fulfilling the mandate God set for me. This innovation came *because* of the pause, and it's a practice that continues to guide me to this day.

It turns out that what they say is true: change of pace + change of place = change of perspective!

Monthly

Once a month I take a full day out to retreat. But this kind of retreating is not about backing down – it's a retreat to advance! I practise silence and solitude, review goals and objectives, and make necessary course adjustments. Again, this is an invaluable time to lift my sights up from the daily whirlwind of getting stuff done to take the long view. Out of these times have come some of my best ideas, biggest dreams and clearest revelations. I shudder to think of the cul-de-sac I would be in were it not for these regular spaces to retreat and reset.

Weekly

Consider building a weekly rhythm of fasting into your schedule; a day each week to give up food (or, if this is not possible for health reasons, something else, like technology for example), and utilize the times you would normally be eating to pray. This is an often forgotten spiritual discipline, but we would do well to remember that Jesus said, '*When* you fast' not '*If* you fast' (Matthew 6.16). If fasting weekly seems like a big step, then just have a go once a month. However you do it, fasting should be an integral part of our discipleship, not an optional add-on for extra credit.

Daily

The daily pause should be less analytical and more devotional; it's about daily centring our lives on Jesus. Like you, my days are often relentless once they get going, and so in addition to taking time to read my Bible and speak to the Lord, I've starting spending five minutes each morning in complete silence, simply loving God and receiving his love. It's wonderful! This moment of stillness before the busyness of the day commences ensures I am able to go through the day aware of God's presence with me.

One last thing on the daily pause. I'm aware that not all of us are morning people, but I've always thought that if Jesus did something it's wise for us to imitate him. Mark's Gospel gives us an insight into Jesus' pattern of prayer: 'Very early in the morning, while it was still dark, Jesus got up, left the house and went off to a solitary place, where he prayed' (Mark 1.35).

So even if you're not naturally a morning person (I wasn't), I'm still going to challenge you to set that alarm a few minutes early and start your day with Jesus. Because, let's be honest, the alternative is usually that we start the day with our phones, scrolling through our Insta feeds, checking email, replying to messages, going down the rabbit hole of notifications and click-throughs. But starting our day in that way is a recipe for hurry, comparison, striving, discontentment and adrenaline-charged overstimulation. So, please, whatever you do, don't spend time with your phone before you've spent some time with Jesus. Take the first moments of your day to centre yourself on his presence and love; this is the pathway to peace, stillness, contentment, wholeness and joy. The way we spend the first moment of our day will influence how we experience every moment of our day – so let's start with Jesus.

Your work with children and young people is way too important to jump from one day to the next without pausing to ensure you are

17

staying on God's agenda. So whatever it looks like for you, if you don't have a strategic, intentional and regular discipline of taking time to pause, reflect and innovate, then put down this book, pick up your diary (or calendar app), get this stuff into your schedule and protect it!

Application questions

- Do any of the dangers discussed in this chapter ring true for you? How will you combat these?
- Create some regular space in your calendar to pause, reflect and innovate. What will you do annually? What will you do monthly? What will you do weekly? What will you do daily?

I TRIED TO SET A CULTURE THAT I DIDN'T MODEL, AND THAT CULTURE WOULD NOT STICK. EXAMPLE IS EVERYTHING.

03
MODEL IT

I was walking through my home town when a parked car caught my attention. Now, I'm no car enthusiast, so this doesn't happen often, but this particular vehicle warranted a second look. Not because it was a dazzling sports car or a beautifully refurbished classic; not even because there was a dog wearing a neckerchief hanging out of the window (sadly), but because of the sheer quantity of bird poo that liberally lathered the vehicle. I mean, we've all parked under a tree and returned to our vehicles to find a nasty surprise on the windscreen, but this was something else – a bird poo paint job, if you will. How, I wondered, could a vehicle owner safely navigate this automobile when no trace of visibility remained through the thickly encrusted windscreen? And then I saw it. A large, bright-yellow advert affixed to the top of the car, proclaiming in big, bold capital letters, 'HAND CAR WASH, THIS WAY'.

That, friends, is not a car wash I will be visiting any time soon!

Having paused to revel in the irony of the moment (it was not a clever marketing ploy to gain the customers attention!), I got to thinking, isn't this sometimes what we do with our leadership in youth and children's ministry? We encourage our young people to develop their personal relationship with God when our own devotional life is intermittent at best. We teach our young people to live lives of purity when our own internet history has recently been 'cleared'. We want our young people to be disciplined in their GCSE revision when we hit the snooze button five times this morning and rolled up for work ten minutes late. We talk to our young people about how important it is to be sharing their faith at school when we shy away from those same conversations with our friends and neighbours. We want to see our young people passionate for Jesus when we're more passionate about our football team. We encourage our children to honour their parents when we go home to constant arguments with our family. Or, to put it another way, we advertise a car wash when we're covered in poo.

But here's the thing: *leadership is primarily about embodying that which we invite others to follow.* The apostle Paul exemplified this principle in his leadership, as we see from his repeated invitations to imitate his way of life: 'Therefore I urge you to imitate me' and 'Follow my example, as I follow the example of Christ' was his invitation to the church in Corinth (1 Corinthians 4.16; 11.1). Likewise, he urged the believers in Philippi: 'Join together in following my example, brothers and sisters, and just as you have us as a model, keep your eyes on those who live as we do' (Philippians 3.17).

I used to think it would be arrogant and presumptuous to say something similar to the people I lead, until I understood that *is* leadership. Example is everything. We have to model it. So let me tell you about a time I got this right, and a time I screwed it up.

A number of years ago I assembled a team to pioneer a new youth ministry for 15–18-year-olds in my home town. After getting involved in the local schools and doing our homework about the area, we launched a new youth club called Limitless Malvern. I knew it was going to be tough going because the church we were working with didn't have a building, and that meant every week would involve shifting a whole load of gear into a venue space, setting it all up, packing it all down and shifting it all back. I knew that in order to make this happen everyone would need to bring the best of their energy and effort from start to finish, and that we would need to keep smiling throughout. And if I wanted that to happen, I would have to model it.

Now, were the team capable of doing all this without me? Very much so. But what would it have communicated if I had expected them to do the leg work while I rocked up at 7.30 for doors? What would that have done for team morale? And what right would I have to challenge anyone in the team for showing up late or not pitching in? Example is everything.

I didn't take my own advice, however, on one of the occasions we took a group of young people on a trip to Laser Quest – the non-lethal war zone that serves as a long-standing youth ministry favourite. At some point in among the usual carnage of running, shooting and sweating, one young person went over on her ankle, so a couple of us took her to A&E just to be sure. Now, you need to know that, as a brand new youth club working largely with unchurched young people, we had decided that one of our 'measurable wins' would be to take the opportunity to pray with young people as often as we could. And this moment in A&E was one such opportunity. I could so easily have offered to pray for healing, but I didn't. I missed it. And I was gutted. I would have expected my team to do it, but I didn't model it. So in our next team meeting I made the point of apologizing to the team because I tried to set a culture that I didn't model, and that culture would not stick. Example is everything.

Simply put, *we cannot ask people to go where we are not willing to go ourselves.* So we must model in our lives what we want to see in the lives of our teams and young people.

In researcher David Kinnaman's excellent book, *You Lost Me*, a young person called Emma was asked what she was looking for in a youth leader. Her answer has lingered with me from the moment I read it:

I want you to be someone I want to grow up like. I want you to step up and live by the Bible's standards. I want you to be inexplicably generous, unbelievably faithful, and radically committed. I want you to be a noticeably better person than my humanist teacher, than my atheist doctor, than my Hindu next-door neighbour. I want you to sell all you have and give it to the poor. I want you to not worry about your health like you're afraid of dying. I want you to live like you actually believe in the God you preach about. I don't want you to be like me; I want you to be like Jesus. That's when I'll start listening.[1]

You should probably read that again.

If you're anything like me, you will be upset and inspired by Emma's challenge in equal measure. Upset because she describes in no uncertain terms the weighty responsibility of leadership. Upset because of the painful reality that I don't always live up to the life of following Jesus I espouse. But inspired once again to live like I actually believe in the God I preach about.

Take a moment to consider: what do you want to see flourish in the lives of your teams, children and young people? A passionate and contagious faith? Model it. A love for the Scriptures? Model it. Faithfulness and a servant heart? Model it. A love for the poor and underprivileged? Model it. Sexual purity in their relationships? Model it. A deep desire for the lost to be found? Model it.

There is simply no escaping the truth that who we are speaks louder than what we say. This is not about perfection, but it is about integrity. It's about not advertising a car wash when our car is covered with poo.

As activist and change-maker Rosa Parks would have it, 'each person must live their life as a model for others'. Example is everything.

Application questions

- What do you long to see in the lives of your children and young people? Are you modelling that in your own life?
- What kind of culture are you trying to create in your team? How are you personally demonstrating what that culture looks like?
- If you were to ask the people you lead to imitate you, would that be a good thing?

WE CANNOT CHOOSE OUR CIRCUMSTANCES, BUT WE CAN CHOOSE OUR RESPONSE TO THOSE CIRCUMSTANCES.

04

CHOOSE YOUR ATTITUDE

We've all had a bad day. Most of us have had a bad week. Some of us have had a bad month. Few of us have had a bad three years. Yet Horatio Spafford experienced exactly that. If you recognize his name it may be because he is the composer of the great old hymn, 'It is well'. The story of how that hymn came about is truly remarkable.

Horatio Spafford was married with four daughters. In 1871 the Great Fire of Chicago destroyed the Spaffords' home. With no insurance to cover them, they lost almost everything they had. So Horatio put his wife and his four children on board a ship to England while he stayed at home to rebuild their livelihood.

A few days after the ship departed, however, he received a telegram from his wife: 'Saved alone. What shall I do?' There had been a shipwreck, and all four of their daughters had drowned in the accident. I cannot imagine anything worse. Which is why what happened next inspires me as much as it astounds me.

Horatio quickly boarded another ship to England. As it passed over the very same place in the ocean where his daughters had been so tragically taken from him, he penned these words:

> When peace like a river attendeth my way,
> when sorrows like sea billows roll;

whatever my lot, thou hast taught me to say,
'It is well, it is well with my soul.'

Wow.

What Horatio's story teaches me is this: we cannot choose our circumstances, but we *can* choose our response to those circumstances. I'm reminded of the prayer of Habakkuk, who said:

Though the fig-tree does not bud
  and there are no grapes on the vines,
though the olive crop fails
  and the fields produce no food,
though there are no sheep in the sheepfold
  and no cattle in the stalls,
yet I will rejoice in the LORD,
  I will be joyful in God my Saviour.
(Habakkuk 3.17–18)

Habakkuk chooses to rejoice and be joyful in God not *because of* his circumstances but *in spite of* them.

I believe that one of the primary responsibilities for a leader is to create a culture of hope. Leaders should be the ones who see the best in the children and young people, who believe that God has a brighter tomorrow for them and encourages them to that end. Leaders believe that even if today has been bad, tomorrow could be better. They lift the spirit of their teams after a difficult Friday night or Sunday morning. They are optimists. They are dreamers. They are visionaries. They create a culture of expectation in their teams by painting a picture of what could be. They 'overflow with hope' (Romans 15.13).

This is why leaders must learn the art of speaking to their soul; of taking control of their emotions rather than allowing their emotions to take control of them. This doesn't mean being fake or disingenuous, it means their attitude is consistent through good times and bad.

So, take a moment to consider: if you've had a bad Friday, how does that come out on a Friday night? Are you downcast and sullen? Are you snappy and short with people? Do you bring the atmosphere of your team down with you? Do your young people give you a wide berth for fear you may bite their hands off? Do you just not show up at all? Or do you choose your attitude? To paraphrase Habakkuk, 'though I've had a really bad day, yet I will bring the best of myself to God and the young people tonight'.

It's therefore important that leaders have someone with whom we are able to be brutally honest, to laugh and cry with, and to vent at when we feel frustrated; a confidant with whom we are able to spill our guts to ensure that we don't spill them over our children and young people. Once we have done that we will be more able to choose our attitude.

Our feelings should be neither ignored nor placed in charge. Jesus offers the perfect demonstration of this principle when his cousin and friend John the Baptist was beheaded on the orders of King Herod. On hearing the news, Jesus withdrew to a solitary place to grieve, which shows us that Jesus was appropriately attentive to his emotions. The crowds, however, didn't respect his need for privacy and followed him anyway (Matthew 14.1–13). The easiest thing for Jesus to have done in this moment would have been to further withdraw or send them away. Surely that's what he wanted to do. But rather than rejecting the crowd, Jesus 'had compassion on them and healed those who were ill' (Matthew 14.14), and then miraculously fed over five thousand of them (Matthew 14.15–21)! Just think, if Jesus had acted in response to his feelings rather than in spite of them, we would have missed out on one of the greatest miracles recorded in all Scripture.

I truly believe that one of the most important things leaders can learn is how to make choices in spite of their feelings rather than because of them. So much of our spiritual growth stems from this discipline. Leadership expert Stephen Covey argues that the ability to choose our response lies at the foundation of what it means to be a proactive person:

> Look at the word responsibility – 'response-ability' – the ability to choose your response. Highly proactive people recognise that responsibility. They do not blame their circumstances, conditions, or conditioning for their behaviour. Their behaviour is a product of their own conscious choice, based on values, rather than a product of their conditions, based on feeling.[1]

We cannot choose our circumstances but we can choose our response to the circumstances. What makes the difference is not the ferocity of the storm but the depth of our character. So choose your attitude. Be overflowing with hope. Create a culture of expectation. Inspire optimism in others when they are close to giving up. For it is to this end that God calls us to lead.

Application questions

- Do you tend to act in response to your emotions or in spite of them? How can you ensure that you are aware of your feelings without placing them in charge?

- Who are the people in your life with whom you can be brutally honest?
- Do your teams, children and young people feel they can be brutally honest with you?

PASSION IS MORE ABOUT PURPOSE THAN VOLUME; MORE ABOUT PERSEVERANCE THAN NOISE.

05
DISCOVER YOUR PASSION

___

If you were feeling unwell today you would find a thermometer and take your temperature. A high temperature would be a sign of ill health. According to the apostle Paul, however, the same cannot be said of our spirituality. On the contrary, the hotter the better!

'Never be lacking in zeal,' writes Paul, 'but keep your spiritual fervour, serving the Lord' (Romans 12.11). The Greek word translated here as 'spiritual fervour' is *zeō*, meaning 'to bubble over because hot enough to boil'.[1]

Another word we might use to describe this kind of spiritual fervour is 'passion'. Passion is the fuel that leaders run on. It is the contagious fire that ignites the hearts of our teams and young people. It is the energy that drives you to get up in the morning and give your best each day. Because when you're passionate about something, no one has to *make* you do it, you *choose* to do it.

The pages of Scripture are littered with leaders who ooze passion. It was passion that motivated Esther to risk her life for her people. It was passion that moved Nehemiah to rebuild the walls of Jerusalem. It was passion that caused David to confront Goliath, and that same passion bled out of his heart through the psalms. It was passion that motivated Paul to take the gospel to the Gentiles, in spite of tremendous persecution. And it was passion that enabled Jesus to set his unwavering course for the cross. These leaders demonstrate that passion will keep you going in the face of frustration and opposition. It is passion that empowers us to do the thing we were created to do.

And passion precedes influence. Think about it. How many times have you watched a TV show, read a book, visited a restaurant or downloaded an app because someone shared passionately their experience of it? When you're around someone who's passionate about something, it's almost impossible not to catch it from them, because passion is contagious.

Now, I know what you're thinking. When we start talking about passion and leadership it immediately brings to mind images of a fiery communicator with sweat on the brow and spittle on the lips! But this is not necessarily a reflection of the kind of zeal to which the apostle Paul is referring in Romans 12, because passion and noise are not the same thing.

In *The Catalyst Leader*, Brad Lomenick writes this of theologian Eugene Peterson: 'Peterson's passion is evident from the moment you meet him. It's a *quiet and subdued passion*, yet unmistakable.'[2] Evidently, passion is more about purpose than volume. Passion is more about perseverance than noise. Passion is more authentically evident in a relentless focus and a contagious spirit than a fist-pumping speech.

The New Living Translation has Romans 12.11 like this: 'Never be lazy, but work hard and serve the Lord enthusiastically.' Understood this way, passion is not primarily evidenced through the raising of our voice, but the relentless pursuit of a God-given calling through faithful, diligent and consistent service to God.

Identifying your passion

I once heard the founder of the A21 Campaign, Christine Caine, say, 'without passion, we cannot do anything'. If that's true, discovering our deepest passions becomes of paramount importance. So how do we go about identifying our passions?

Passion is usually revealed in our biggest dreams and deepest frustrations. As business consultant Jim Collins writes, 'You can't manufacture passion or "motivate" people to feel passionate. You can only discover what ignites your passion and the passions of those around you.'[3]

The following application questions are designed to do exactly that! Properly considered, these questions have the power to dig beneath the surface of your life and reveal your most heartfelt passions. But be warned, they cannot be seriously answered with a skim-read. So put on a brew, grab your notepad, turn off your phone and invite the Holy Spirit to speak to you as you slowly reflect.

If God made us on purpose, for a purpose, then chances are the things he made us passionate about are the things he is calling us to do something about. So find your passion. Pursue your passion. And lead with passion.

Application questions
- What has been a consistent theme throughout the changing circumstances of your life?
- What skills come to you naturally?
- What would you do for nothing? If you didn't have to worry about money, what would you be doing?
- What's something that, when immersed in it, you lose track of time?

- What gets your blood boiling? What is a problem in the world that you'd love to fix?
- Which activities and results bring you the most joy?
- What are the things that get you up in the morning and keep you awake at night?
- What are the things that, when you do them, you get a sense of 'I was born for this'?

PEOPLE WANT TO FOLLOW A LEADER WHO IS OVERFLOWING, NOT ONE WHO IS OVERSTRETCHED.

06
PASSION KILLERS

I once attended a conference where one speaker was so zealous about her message that she had to fight through the tears to communicate it. It was by no means the most polished message of the event, nor the most well researched or revelatory – but it was the only one that received a standing ovation. Why? Without doubt it was her passion. It was passion that moved her to tears, and passion that gripped the conference floor as we sat compelled by her every word. It was her passion that spread like a contagion through the audience and, ultimately, passion that caused people to get to their feet and applaud. This is the power of passion.

I am deeply stirred by the words of the Episcopal priest Robert Cappon, who asked:

> What happened to the radical Christianity that turned the world upside down? What happened to the category-smashing, life-threatening, anti-institutional gospel that spread through the first century like wildfire? And was considered by those in power – 'dangerous'? What happened to the kind of Christians whose hearts were on fire, who had no fear, who spoke the truth no matter what the consequence; who made the world uncomfortable; who were willing to follow Jesus wherever he went? What happened to the kind of Christians who were filled with passion and gratitude and who, every day, were unable to get over the grace of God?[1]

I don't know about you, but I want to be that kind of Christian. I don't want my faith to be tame, tepid and mundane, but wild, fierce and passionate! I want to be the kind of leader who keeps his passion levels filled up to overflowing, that others might catch something of Jesus from me.

Which is easy to write, but hard to live out. Why? Because passion leaks. I am confronted daily with potential 'passion killers' that un-addressed will cause passion to diminish and retreat in my life. I have come to believe that keeping our spiritual fervour has as much to do with what we tear down as what we turn up. So let's reflect on nine potential 'passion killers' that, if left unidentified and con-fronted, could rob us of our zeal.

Disconnection

I make no apology for continually returning to the primacy of daily time with God throughout this book. And I return to it again here because, make no mistake, the primary way to lose your passion is to lose your time with God. There is a direct correlation between our proximity and our passion: the closer we are to God, the hotter our passion boils, but distance diminishes our passion. Prayer-less people cut themselves off from the refreshing, renewing power of God's presence, the result of which is the all-too-familiar feeling of being beaten down, depleted, overwhelmed and out of control. When this happens, the things we once did joyfully begin to feel like chores as our passion starts to fade.

Conversely, it's when we're close to God that our vision is clearer, our resilience stronger, our courage greater and our passion more contagious. It's when we're close to him that our soul comes alive! Prayer has a way of fanning the flame of spiritual fervour in our souls. Simply put, we cannot live *for* God if we don't connect *with* God.

Comparison

We all know about it, yet we inevitably still fall for it! Comparison is one of the most common passion killers because, in an age of social media, we compare our beginnings to everyone else's endings; our worst bits to everyone else's best bits. But when we allow comparison to get the better of us, we cease to pursue the passions that run through our veins because we convince ourselves that someone else is already doing it better. As we look longingly at somebody else's successes, we begin to journey outside our assigned place in God; we try to run somebody else's race, we try to grow in somebody else's gifts, we try to imitate someone else's assignment, and in doing so we move from joy to discontentment, from passion to frustration, because we cannot be passionate about a calling that God did not create us for. So how do we avoid this passion killer? Seek to be the best version of yourself, not a poor imitation of someone else. Compare yourself to who you were yesterday, not to who someone else is today.

Cynicism

Cynicism is the antithesis of passion. It is equally contagious but entirely destructive; it will destroy the passion in you and in those you lead. Cynicism reveals itself in sarcasm and negativity, where passion is revealed in encouragement and hope. And I know which leader I'd rather be!

We should not, however, confuse cynicism with doubt. 'A faith without some doubts', as Pastor Tim Keller once tweeted, 'is like a body without any anti-bodies. It is susceptible to attack.' Doubt, it turns out, can be a good thing for faith because it causes us to ask deeper questions and find more solid answers. But not so with cynicism. Cynicism is the ugly child of pessimism and scepticism. It always chooses to assume the worst, and eats away at us like a slow-release poison. We must do all we can to eliminate cynicism from our teams, our ministries and our lives.

I recognize the toxicity of cynicism, but this by no means makes me immune. For most of us it's a *when* not an *if*. What's important, then, is how we respond when cynicism begins to take hold. It happened most recently for me when I allowed a number of frustrations that seemed small in isolation to get on top of me and, as is so often the case, cynicism is born in frustration left untended.

When I realized that my frustration had begun to migrate into cynicism, I took some time out with God to face it head on. As I examined my heart I made a list in my journal of each of the things that were aggravating me, reflecting on each, one by one. I made a fire in the wood burner at the retreat centre I was visiting and cast each frustration into the flame, giving it to God as I went. I went back to my journal, this time making a list of all the things I was grateful for, all the responsibilities I am privileged to enjoy, thanking God for the many blessings he has generously and graciously poured into my life. The result? My circumstances didn't change, but my *perspective* on the circumstances most certainly did. Cynicism was replaced with hope, and passion was rekindled in my heart again.

As a leader, you must be ruthless in your battle against cynicism. Do not stand for it! Build your ministry by having a contagious passion, not a destructive cynicism. Be passionate about what God has called you to do, not cynical about what he has called someone else to do.

Losing your why

You didn't get into youth or children's ministry for the pay packet (can I get an Amen?). You didn't get into it for the status, the job title or the glory, because there's not too much of that going around. You didn't get into this because you were just desperate to work evenings and weekends and to spend your summers in a tent. No. You chose those things willingly because *your passion outweighed the sacrifice.* You got into this in spite of those things, because you were boiling over for Jesus, and bubbling up with passion for passing on the gospel to a generation who so desperately needed to hear it.

But then something happened, and it happened so incrementally that you barely noticed it. You got so consumed with *what* you were doing that you forgot *why* you were doing it. You filled in one too many risk assessments, took one too many Saturdays away from your family, had a few too many misunderstandings with your line manager, had a few too many behavioural issues to deal with . . . and the 'why' that once so consumed you – to pass on the gospel to the next generation – slowly began to get lost under a pile of consent forms. And now, if you're really honest, the spiritual fervour that once compelled you to do anything for the gospel is not quite as bubbling up and boiling over as it once was.

If that's you, this would be a good moment to remind yourself of Jesus' invitation to come back to your first love. Remind yourself of your 'why' – the reason you got into this in the first place – and allow that passion to be rekindled in your heart again.

Distraction

One of my favourite stories of passionate leadership in Scripture is that of Nehemiah. While living in exile in Babylon, Jerusalem had been left lying in ruins. Hearing of this, Nehemiah's passion is so greatly stirred he is moved to tears, and sets about gathering a team to rebuild the walls. His opponents try all kinds of tactics to derail the plan, but nothing works. So they resort to a tactic so many of us fall for – *distraction*. Nehemiah's opponents call him to a meeting! But Nehemiah's passion is so great that he will not allow himself to be distracted. He is intently focused on that which God has called him to do, so simply retorts, 'I am doing a great work and I cannot come down' (Nehemiah 6.3, ESV).

Distraction diminishes our passion because it burdens our lives and fills them with surplus activities the Lord never assigned to us. I love the way author and contemplative Brennan Manning accurately diagnoses this problem in his powerful book, *The Signature of Jesus*:

> Our days become a never-ending succession of appointments, committee meetings, burdens, and responsibilities . . . Weary and breathless, we sense that life is slipping away. We change our wardrobe, slip into the costume for our next performance, and regret that we have tasted so little of the peace and joy that Jesus promised.[2]

We must not allow distraction – be that Fortnite, Fifa, Netflix, or even unnecessary meetings – to rob us of pursuing the passions God has placed on our hearts, because, as Pastor Erwin McManus says, 'There are few things more powerful than a life lived with passionate clarity.'[3]

When you kill time, it has no resurrection! The time we lose to scrolling through Facebook is not coming back. So let's avoid re-treating into time-wasters and 'busywork', and give the best of our time and energy to the things that make us come alive.

Overstretched

If you were to go to the gym periodically you would *build* a muscle. If you were to go to the gym ceaselessly you would *strain* that muscle.

Being stretched in short periods is a good thing; it causes us to depend on God, increase our capacity and grow stronger as a result. Indeed, you have to be stretched to be strengthened.

But stay in that overstretched zone over time and things begin to break down. Without time to rest and replenish we become tired and depleted. Our days get longer and our fuses get shorter. As our margins decrease so does our spiritual vitality. We lose our joy, and our passion erodes. We spend so much of ourselves on our work, without realizing that the very thing we must cultivate to do that work – our passion – is diminishing.

People want to follow a leader who is overflowing, not one who is overstretched. Be careful, then, that the pace at which you are doing God's work is not destroying God's work in you.

Underchallenged

While it's true that an overstretched muscle will strain, it is also true that an underused muscle will atrophy. The same is true of our passion. When we are underchallenged we get bored and sleepy, we stop taking risks and find ourselves stuck in the rut of routine as our passion ebbs away. So to keep our passion hot we must continually exercise it by casting visions that scare us and working hard to achieve them.

If your passion is not boiling hot right now then please hear this: the fastest way to wake you up from the routine and set your passion bubbling again is to go after something *for* God that you cannot possibly accomplish *without* God.

Has everything become too easy for you? Do you pretty much know what you're doing? Have you got it covered with your skill set and resources? Then now is the time to turn it up. Dream a new dream.

Pray a more audacious prayer. Go after a compelling vision. And watch as passion begins to peak in your life again.

Cold companions

Having spent a few months out on the road preparing for a half marathon, I had a pretty good idea from the training runs of the time I might achieve come race day. You can imagine my surprise, then, when my actual finish time was far quicker than I had anticipated! So what happened? Because I surely had not become miraculously fitter overnight. In fact, the explanation is simple. In training I was running on my own, but during the race there were a whole load of people running faster than me and I was trying to keep up!

One of the main reasons we lose our passion is because we are not running with passionate people. Conversely, those who surround themselves with passionate people tend to turn up the dial on their own spiritual intensity. I love the way Pastor Mark Batterson reflects this principle:

> I need people around me who make me feel small because their dreams are so big. I need to be around people who make me feel far from God because they're so close to Jesus. I need to be around people who make me feel as if I'm doing next to nothing because they're making such a big difference.[4]

The truth is, we ultimately reflect those with whom we surround ourselves, and passionate people produce passionate people. As founder of Starbucks, Howard Schultz, says, 'When you're surrounded by people who share a collective passion for a common purpose, anything is possible.'[5] So get yourself a band of brothers and sisters who are running faster and burning hotter than you, and watch as your temperature gauge goes into the red!

Underestimating significance

Attempting to pass the time on a long-haul flight, I started watching the movie *Fighting with My Family*. I figured that if it's got The Rock in it, it must be good. Am I right? Anyway . . . I was enjoying it, if a little dazed and confused from far too many hours on a plane, but my attention was immediately piqued when I heard one of the characters say, 'Just because millions of people aren't cheering when you do it, doesn't mean it's not important.' They weren't talking about youth and children's ministry (they were actually talking about wrestling) but they really could have been.

It will not have escaped your attention that youth and children's ministry is sometimes overlooked and undervalued in the Church. Too often it is seen as a stepping stone into adult ministry, or a training ground in which people can learn until they 'step up' into the 'real thing'. The danger with this nonsense is that this narrative has become so deeply engrained in church culture that you actually believe it and begin to internalize it. You become convinced that your ministry is of secondary importance, and you lose your passion as you look to do something more notable. But if that's you, I'm afraid you have been deceived.

You see, during your lifetime you may well do something *other* than youth or children's ministry. You could do something that is more public or impressive. You could do something that is held in higher esteem by the Church. You could surely do something that pays you more, or has a better career path. But please hear me now – *you will never do something more important.*

I simply cannot conceive of anything more necessary that you could give your life to than passing on the gospel to the next generation. So keep going. Do not lose your passion, because what you are doing is of absolute, paramount importance!

Leader, may I encourage you, never apologize for your passion. Don't bottle it up, don't water it down – turn it up! Paint vivid pictures of the future you envision for your children and young people. Let the love of Jesus in you flow out unfiltered. Let your passion for the lost spill over so that the people around you can't help but catch it. Let the fire in your belly translate into the sound of your voice as you communicate. And never be lacking in zeal, but keep your spiritual fervour, serving the Lord.

Application questions

- On a scale of 1–10, how 'bubbling up and boiling over' is your passion right now? What changes might be necessary in order to turn it up?
- Which of the potential passion killers is most likely to erode your spiritual fervour? What might you need to do to combat it?

HUMBLE LEADERS ARE A LAUNCH PAD FOR OTHERS TO SPRING FROM, RATHER THAN A CEILING THEY CAN'T BREAK THROUGH.

07

HUMBLE LEADERS ARE BETTER LEADERS

Which single characteristic do you think is common to the most successful business leaders in the world? Great charisma, clear vision, articulate communication, burning passion, thick skin, a ruthless streak? None of the above!

In his seminal work *Good to Great*, Jim Collins and his research team explored the nature of the top executives in the business world. They researched companies who outperformed the rest of the market by (on average) seven times for a sustained period of 15 years. They were astonished by their discovery:

> We were surprised, shocked really, to discover the type of leadership required for turning a good company into a great one. Compared to high-profile leaders with big personalities who make headlines and become celebrities, the good-to-great leaders seem to have come from Mars. Self-effacing, quiet, reserved, even shy – these leaders are a paradoxical blend of personal humility and professional will . . . We found leaders of this type at the helm of every good-to-great company.[1]

To their surprise, humility was the characteristic that marked out these 'great' leaders from the rest. They described it as a shocking discovery, and yet we really should have known all along. The greatest leader to have ever walked the earth,

> did not consider equality with God
> something to be used to his own advantage;
> rather, he made himself nothing
> by taking the very nature of a servant,
> being made in human likeness.
> And being found in appearance as a man,
> he humbled himself
> by becoming obedient to death –
> even death on a cross!
> (Philippians 2.6–8)

Yet his humility did nothing to diminish his influence. On the contrary, thousands of years later, billions of people across the globe still follow his lead. Humble leaders, it seems, are better leaders. Here's why . . .

Humble leaders learn more quickly

Humble leaders will learn and grow at a rate that the proud have no hope of doing. This is because humble leaders open themselves up to the idea of being wrong, receiving correction and asking others how they think it could be done better. They learn from people regardless of their status, stature or age. They reflect on their practice and are quick to learn from their mistakes. Conversely, arrogant leaders tend to over-evaluate their performance, fail to listen adequately to the people around them, and shy away from engaging with hard truths – all of which conspires to bypass the opportunity for learning.

In his book *The Five Dysfunctions of a Team*,[2] business consultant Patrick Lencioni argues that one of the main factors that restricts growth is 'lack of conflict' in a team. While this may sound counter-intuitive on first hearing, Lencioni suggests that healthy teams have enough trust to say what they are really thinking and feeling. Without this, teams lack honest reflection and constructive criticism, which in turn stunts growth.

When you approach your teams and young people with humility, they experience validation. They experience your interest in what they think. They feel valued because your listening ear communicates that you believe they have something unique and significant to contribute. This encourages open and robust conversation where team members and young people feel free to say it as they see it, rather than holding back on their true opinion for fear of upsetting the leader. Easily offended leaders with inflated egos do not encourage honest teams. Allowing constructive criticism and encouraging it at a team level is a powerful way to learn quickly, but it requires a humble leader to create this culture.

Humble leaders get the best from those they lead

Humble leaders are a launch pad for others to spring from, rather than a ceiling they can't break through. They take delight in those who were once 'below' them going on to bigger and better things than they have ever achieved. And herein lies the nature of true leadership: not to grow in personal influence but to maximize the potential in others – which inevitably demands they get the credit! When our ego prevents us from relinquishing the spotlight, we become the ceiling that our teams and young people will never surpass. But humble leaders create the opportunity for others to thrive.

Humble leaders engender loyalty

Humble leaders are quick to admit their mistakes, which – contrary to popular belief – strengthens a leader's reputation. (We'll discuss this in more detail in Chapter 15, 'The paradox of apology'.) Their authentic vulnerability communicates that they too are imperfect humans. This endears people to the leader because, while their strengths may impress people, their vulnerabilities *connect* with them. Simply put, they are more likeable. This is why humble leaders engender loyalty in those they lead.

Humble leaders are more persuasive

Much of leadership in youth and children's ministry is about our power of persuasion. We are constantly seeking to persuade people to join our teams, give financially towards our next residential, release funds for our programmes, engage in our weekly Bible studies, or bring a friend on Friday night. The humble are more persuasive than the arrogant, because the key weapon in the arsenal of the persuader is their *character*. Arrogance is a deterrent, where genuine humility has a way of winning others over.

Humble leaders are fearless leaders

The fear of failure is often rooted in a fear of losing face, but if you fear failure you stunt innovation. Humble leaders are more comfortable in taking calculated risks because the progress of the ministry is more important than the preservation of their reputation. So humble leaders don't look after their reputation; they look after their character and their reputation looks after itself. Humble leaders establish an environment where it's OK to try and fail – as long as you try. Thus humility cultivates courage, and courage cultivates progress.

Humble leaders have God on their side!

When Scripture says something once, you know it's true. When Scripture repeats that truth over and over, you know you'd better pay attention! There is a special significance, then, when Scripture repeats 'God opposes the proud but shows favour to the humble' three times (Proverbs 3.34; James 4.6; 1 Peter 5.5). And no wonder – it's a massive statement! If we lack humility, God actually stands *against* us. I don't know about you, but that's not a position I ever want to find myself in. Conversely, humble leaders are better leaders because they attract the favour of God. Wonderful! So, 'Humble yourselves before the Lord, and he will lift you up' (James 4.10).

My experience is that the people I lead and serve are often far more courageous and creative than me. Given the right environment, their contributions can be world-changing for our ministries, if we only have the humility to listen.

Application questions
- Think of the leaders you most admire. Would you describe them as humble?
- Are you approachable and open to challenge?
- How readily do you listen to and learn from people with less experience or status than you?
- Do you quickly admit your mistakes, or do you try to cover them up to save face?

THE MOMENT YOU PUT YOUR FINGERS IN YOUR EARS YOU PUT A CEILING ON YOUR GROWTH.

08

SOAK IT UP: THE ART OF RECEIVING FEEDBACK

It won't have escaped your attention that everyone in your church has an opinion about your youth and children's ministry, right? Your senior leaders have an opinion, your young people have an opinion, the parents of your children have an opinion, your spouse definitely has an opinion . . . and very often those opinions are 'suggestions' for how you might do things differently. The way you respond to these suggestions, even criticisms, will determine how much you learn and grow. There are three ways we typically respond to feedback, well meaning or otherwise.

Option 1: The wasp

Whenever anyone shares an alternative view, you are quickly provoked and strike back. You go on the defensive, giving an immediate retort; a long list of reasons as to why you do it this way and why it still remains the best way. In this instance, instead of *listening* you are *defending* your process, method, programme and so on.

Option 2: The hedgehog

You curl up in a ball and hide from it. Unlike the wasp, you don't lash back with a retort, and thus give the impression you are listening, but you are figuratively putting your fingers in your ears. This happens when you confuse a criticism about *what you do* with a personal slight about *who you are*. So to avoid feeling hurt you try to let it bounce off you and forget about it as soon as possible.

Option 3: The sponge

You soak it up. Your posture is hands open rather than arms crossed. You are wise enough to receive feedback from every angle, even those who may be significantly less experienced and knowledgeable in your field. You are discerning enough to know that in almost every criticism there exists a nugget of truth if you would be humble enough to seek it out. And because you are always listening, you are always learning.

That's why the wise King Solomon once said, 'The way of fools seems right to them, but the wise listen to advice' (Proverbs 12.15). Conversely, the moment you put your fingers in your ears you put a ceiling on your growth.

The level to which you limit feedback is the level to which you limit growth. So how can you actively gather constructive feedback?

360-degree feedback

Imagine a compass with you in the middle. In your role as a youth or children's worker you will have leadership relationships with people at every degree on the compass. North are your senior leaders. East and west are your peers; perhaps other staff members at your church or the parents of your young people. And south are the children and team members you lead. And because each of these groups sees you from a different angle, they each have a different perspective and thus a uniquely valuable perspective. So 360-degree feedback is the art of seeking out the thoughts of people from every angle.

North. This may take the form of a weekly meeting with your senior leader and a more in-depth annual performance review. If you don't have either of these things, ask for them. Take the initiative. Invite your senior leaders to come and observe your youth or children's group. Ask them to watch how you lead your team, preach your message and engage with your children and young people. They may not be youth or children's workers, but they will have a unique perspective which, if you seek it out, could be a catalyst for growth.

East/west. What do the parents of your children and young people think? What do their kids feed back to them after a Sunday morning at Children's Church or a Friday night at youth? Have they managed to internalize the message of the session? Did they have a good time? This is a perspective that only the parents will have and will remain elusive to you unless you actively seek it out.

South. The best people to offer feedback for your children's or youth ministry are your children and young people! But are you listening? At our youth group in Malvern, we've made it a priority to listen to those we lead. We will consult our young people about the content of our sessions and the trips we go on together. At the end of the academic year we even ask all of our young people to fill out a feedback form with questions like, 'Do you feel welcome and valued? Do you feel free to be yourself? Do you feel more open to God than when you started coming? What is one thing you would change?' and so on. Perhaps that sounds boring, but it demonstrates to your young people that you value them enough to care about their opinion.

Remember, the moment you put your fingers in your ears you put a ceiling on your growth. So don't be a wasp or a hedgehog – be a sponge! Actively go in search of constructive feedback from every angle and soak it up. Listen. Respond. Grow.

Application questions

- When was the last time you sought feedback from the people around you? If it's been a while, why not embark on a 360-degree feedback exercise. You could ask your young people to fill in a feedback form, and send out a questionnaire to the parents of your children or young people. You could ask your senior leader to come and observe a session and arrange a follow-up meeting afterwards to gather their feedback. You may not agree with everything that's said, but you're sure to learn a lot.

THE LEADERS WHO MAKE THE BIGGEST IMPACT ARE NOT NECESSARILY THE ONES WHO ARE THE MOST GIFTED, BUT THOSE WHO ARE THE MOST RESILIENT.

09

HOW TO KEEP GOING WHEN YOU FEEL LIKE GIVING UP

Have you ever felt like giving up?

You know, the time when no one showed up to your youth group; or when that fight kicked off; or when your senior leaders said no to your big vision? Or perhaps it was when all your key team members stepped down at once; when the amount of work seemed insurmountable and overwhelming; or when the kids in your children's ministry just would not listen, no matter what you tried. Whatever it was, it left you wondering, 'What's the point? I can't do this any more!'

OK – so let me rephrase the question: *when* was the last time you felt like giving up?

Although I will never know the name and story of everyone who reads this book, I am confident that we all share this one thing in common: we have each gone through moments where the thought of quitting was much more attractive than the proposition of pressing on. We have *all* been through times when we felt like giving up.

With that said, I am equally confident of this: at the end of our lives, we won't remember the things that came easy; we'll remember the things that came hard. And if I have learned one thing from the years I've been following Jesus, it's this: *the greatest things in life are always the ones that cost us the most.*

This is why the leaders who make the biggest impact are not necessarily the ones who are the most gifted, but those who are the most resilient. As the author of Hebrews reminds us, 'You need to persevere so that when you have done the will of God, you will receive what he has promised' (Hebrews 10.36). Perseverance precedes the promise! Could it be that the purposes of God for your life are on the other side of the wall you just hit?

We all want to 'receive what he has promised'. The problem is, 'You need to persevere' is easier said than done. So, how do we keep going when we feel like giving up? What are the practical steps we can take to build resilience into our lives and ministries?

Truth-loading

Back in 2013 I ran the London Marathon. In preparation, I was advised to spend a week prior to the race 'carb-loading'. The idea is to store up a reserve of glycogen in your muscles, so that when your strength has gone and energy is depleted, your body has a reserve it can call upon to help you to keep moving when you feel like giving up.

Youth and children's ministry is very much a marathon. And if we are to persevere we need to apply a similar principle: to store up a reserve – not of carbohydrate but of truth. 'Truth-loading' is about creating a catalogue, in writing, of the promises of God over our lives. These could be truths from Scripture, specific prophetic words that have been spoken over you, moments where you have seen God move in and through you, or the key times when you heard the call of God over your life, so that when the time comes that you feel like throwing in the towel, you have a reserve that you can go back to and call upon to give you the strength to persevere.

Victor Raymond Edman once said, 'never doubt in the dark what God told you in the light', which is true, but much easier to do if you have stored up what God told you in the light so you can call upon it when the darkness comes.

Practise gratitude

The easiest thing to do when we feel like giving up is to fixate on all the things that are bad about our situation. If we're not careful, we can become consumed by self-pity, and the deeper into that hole we go, the dimmer the light of hope becomes. But hope is the fuel that leadership runs on. When leaders lose hope, they forfeit their capacity to lead.

Gratitude is the weapon that pushes back against the forces of self-pity. Gratitude is like a war cry in difficulty that declares, 'I will not be consumed!' But let me be clear: cultivating an attitude of gratitude isn't about pretending nothing is bad; it's about choosing to focus your attention on what's good. It's about choosing to get up each morning and count your blessings; to remind yourself of the goodness of God and, in doing so, hold on to hope.

Rightly measure success

Part of the reason that we find ourselves on the edge of giving up is because we have a misappropriated metric for measuring success. When no one shows up, or the fight kicks off, or the vision gets shut down, or no one listens to our talk, we equate that with failure. We can handle feeling like a failure once or twice, but over time our inner narrative changes from 'I failed' to 'I am a failure'. And that's when we give up. But let me give you a new (biblical) way to measure success.

Did you do what God asked you to do, and did you give it everything you've got? If the answer is 'Yes', congratulations, you're a success, and God can use you.

Remember Jesus

The author of Hebrews instructs us that if we ever feel like giving up, we should remember what Jesus endured on our behalf and take heart:

> let us run with perseverance the race marked out for us, fixing our eyes on Jesus, the pioneer and perfecter of our faith. For the joy that was set before him he endured the cross, scorning its shame, and sat down at the right hand of the throne of God. Consider him who endured such opposition from sinners, so that you will not grow weary and lose heart. (Hebrews 12.1–3)

If you find yourself in a moment where you feel like giving up, remember Jesus, who has already run the race and overcome, who persevered and made it across the finishing line. Let that thought be the central motivation for you to persevere. If you feel like giving up, remember that Jesus didn't give up on you, even though it cost him everything.

I once heard Mike Pilavachi say it like this: 'God can use a failure, but he can't use a quitter. Get up, keep going. Don't give up. Perseverance is the missing gift in today's Church.'

So please, leader, don't give up now. Don't back down. Keep going! Fix your eyes on Jesus and finish the race he marked out for you.

I am inspired by the apostle Paul, who, towards the end of his life, penned these words:

> I have fought the good fight, I have finished the race, I have kept the faith. Now there is in store for me the crown of right-eousness, which the Lord, the righteous Judge, will award to me on that day – and not only to me, but also to all who have longed for his appearing.
> (2 Timothy 4.7–8)

Please, Lord, may it be that I can echo those words at the end of my days.

Application questions

- Are you doing what God has asked you to do, and are you giving it everything you've got?
- Do you have a written record of the things God has spoken over your life? If not, start today! Begin by writing down all the specific Scriptures, prophetic words and significant moments you can remember, and then keep it updated as your journey continues.
- Take a moment to write a list of everything you are thankful for. Use this list to inspire a moment of praise and thanksgiving, and return to it when challenges and frustrations begin to overwhelm you.
- Open your Bible to one of the Gospels and read again through the Passion narrative. How can Jesus' persever-ance inspire resilience in you today?

TAKE CONTROL OF YOUR SOCIAL MEDIA BEFORE IT TAKES CONTROL OF YOU.

10

THE NEW RULES OF SOCIAL MEDIA

Social media is a helpful tool for youth leaders in particular. It enables us to communicate with our young people in their native, digital language – with appropriate safeguarding measures in place, of course. We can utilize it pastorally, as well as keeping our young people connected with relevant information throughout the week. We can use groups to build community. We can encourage our young people by sharing songs, teaching videos and passages from Scripture. Social media has unlocked a whole new world of instant, real-time interaction and information so, at its best and used well, social media can be a useful tool. But . . . there is a dark side.

When British Youth for Christ asked 1,000 young people to describe the main negative influence on their lives, social media came out on top, with 67 per cent saying it had a more negative impact on them than anything, or anyone, else.[1] And it's not just young people – all of us have felt the impact on our lives. So what is it about social media that makes it so destructive?

Time

Social media is a black hole for time. On average in the UK, we each spend nearly two months of our year online, which is more time than we spend asleep.[2] By my maths, this means that if you are just an average phone user, and you were to continue as you are now for the next 60 years, you would have spent ten years of your life on your phone. It's truly frightening to consider how much better we could invest those ten years than scrolling through our social feeds.

Truth be told, most of us have no idea how much of our time is sucked up by this looming black hole, for the very reason that few of us sit down for hours at a time with phone in hand. Rather, it's the text here, the notification there, the click-through here, the swipe-left there. One recent study showed that the average iPhone user touches their phone 2,617 times a day.[3] In isolation a few minutes pass by, but together these minutes add up to many more hours than we'd like to admit.

Remember, when you kill time it has no resurrection. There is no getting back the time your phone stole from you. If there was ever a case of 'just because everyone's doing it doesn't make it right', surely this is it.

Addiction

Part of the reason we lose so much of our time to our phones and social channels is because the apps we use have been deliberately designed for attention and addiction. The first President of Facebook, Sean Parker, became so disenfranchised with what social media is doing to us that he now describes himself as a 'conscientious objector'. In one interview, Parker gave this frightening glimpse behind the curtain:

> God only knows what it's doing to our children's brains. The thought process that went into building these applications, Facebook being the first of them . . . was all about: 'How do we consume as much of your time and conscious attention as possible?' And that means we need to give you a little dopamine

hit every once in a while because someone commented on your photo or a post or whatever.[4]

The hard reality is that most of us exhibit signs of compulsion, even full-blown addiction, when it comes to our relationship with our phones. As I reflect on this I am reminded of the words the apostle Paul wrote to the church in Corinth: '"I have the right to do anything," you say – but not everything is beneficial. "I have the right to do anything" – but I will not be mastered by anything' (1 Corinthians 6.12).

He wrote these words long before social media was a thing, of course, but it's as if he could have been addressing the issue directly. We certainly have the *right* to use social media, but is it always *beneficial*? Is it benefiting our relationship with God and the people around us? Is it benefiting our mental and emotional well-being? And if it's not, what should we do about it?

Sleep

On average, 91 per cent of young people go to bed with their devices.[5] This is a problem for two reasons: first, because our phones emit something called blue light, which inhibits our levels of melatonin, the chemical that tells our brains we need to sleep, making it harder to go to sleep when we try to. And, second, if we keep our phones switched on and next to our beds at night, notifications and alerts will at least stir us, if not fully wake us. This is a problem because our sleep works in cycles, so when our sleep is disrupted by our phones we have to start that sleep cycle all over again, meaning that we rarely enjoy a full, deep, restorative sleep. This is why parents of young children are always exhausted. One study expresses the challenges this continual interruption creates in this way:

Electronic devices and social media seem to have an especially strong ability to disrupt sleep . . . Sleep deprivation is linked to myriad issues, including compromised thinking and reasoning, susceptibility to illness, weight gain, and high blood pressure. It also affects mood: People who don't sleep enough are prone to depression and anxiety.[6]

Evidently, not getting enough sleep is a big deal. Imagine how many of these related issues we could begin to overcome simply by sorting out our sleep patterns. Some simple adjustments to our life rhythms could have a truly transformative impact.

Mental health

A study published in the journal *Computers and Human Behaviour* found that people who report using seven or more social media platforms were more than three times as likely as people using up to two platforms to have high levels of general anxiety symptoms. A similar study, involving 1,700 people, found a threefold risk of depression and anxiety among people who used the most social media platforms.[7]

Why is this the case? Perhaps the biggest problem is that social media is rarely an accurate representation of our lives. Life is about ups and downs, wins and losses, strengths and weaknesses, joys and sorrows, good days and bad days, successes and failures. That's everyone's story. But it's not our Instagram story. If our social feeds were to be believed, life looks like a glorious procession of ups, wins, strengths, joys, good days and successes. It appears as though everyone is better looking than us, more fashionable than us, more successful than us and more popular than us. But they're not – it's just that we're comparing our blooper reel to everyone else's highlight reel!

The other issue is created by the fact that we're always switched on and plugged in. It's impossible to keep up with everything that's happening on our Snapchat, YouTube, Insta, Tik Tok, Messenger, What's App . . . even writing it is exhausting! We are overloaded with information and stimulation. Silence, solitude, reflection and peace have become a thing of the past as we have developed the habit of automatically reaching for our phones and checking our social channels whenever a moment of downtime presents itself.

So what's the answer? Should we delete all of our social media apps and become technology free? Not necessarily. As I said up front, social media can be a useful tool when we use it right. It's also the primary way our young people communicate, where they are connected and how they are shaped, so it's important to consider how we utilize this tool to make a positive kingdom impact. That's why, instead of asking you to become a digital hermit, I've developed five 'new rules' to help you take control of your social media before it takes control of you.

1 Social media curfew

First up, I want to suggest a self-imposed social media curfew every night. Sounds crazy – right? But nobody ever made a difference by being like everyone else! A social media cut-off every night will allow you to take a break from the pressures of inaccurate comparison and be content with who you are. It will also give you time away from the blue light that emanates from your phone screen tricking your brain into thinking it's daytime, enabling you to get better sleep. That's why I'd suggest you set your personal curfew at least a full hour before you go to bed, after which you will not check your socials or use your phone at all. At first this was a discipline for me, now it's a joy. I feel a tangible sense of relief when I finally get to put my phone on aeroplane mode and shut down for the night. As my phone goes off, my senses come alive. I breathe more deeply and walk more slowly. What a gift! Go on, give it a try. It will be really hard at first, but you'll be glad you did in the end.

2 Social media Sabbath

If you thought that was crazy, try this: a whole 24-hour period without using social media every week. The principle of the Sabbath has been practised by God's people for thousands of years, and I believe this same principle can be applied to the much more modern phenomenon of social media. This extended period of rest from the constant noise and ceaseless digital connection of social media will create an opportunity for you to be totally present to yourself, to your thoughts, to others and to God. This has been my practice for a number of years now and I cannot overemphasize how good it has been for me. It has helped me to mentally rest in a deeper and fuller way. It is a life-giving practice that I would encourage every reader to go for.

3 Turn off notifications

Make your phone your servant not your master by turning your notifications off so that it only has your attention when *you need it*, not when *it needs you*. This will enable you to be more present to the moment, more available to the people around you, and more able to focus on the important tasks that you really want to give your time to.

4 Got a moment? Count to ten

Psychologists are suggesting that, just as pianists wire into their muscle memory how to play a chord through multiple repetitions, we have wired our muscle memory to automatically reach for the phone in our pocket when even the briefest moment of downtime presents itself. It has literally become a reflex. So before reaching for your phone, try counting slowly to ten. Make yourself present to what God is doing and saying in the moment, ensuring that you are only reaching for your phone out of intention rather than habit.

5 Think before you post

We've all had that experience of firing something up online in the heat of the moment that in the cold light of day we lived to regret. We can laugh, but misguided Tweets and thoughtless Snaps regularly lead to hurt, embarrassment and damaged relationships. That's why I'm encouraging you to take a moment to consider the following questions before posting:

Am I seeking affirmation?

When you get a 'like' it releases a chemical called dopamine, which controls the pleasure systems in your brain. The more likes we get, the better we feel about ourselves, and it's highly addictive. So we can fall into the trap of posting the kind of things that we know are going to get us likes. We crave likes because they make us feel loved. But if we are posting to gain affirmation, our personal sense of self-worth becomes rooted in what others think of us, rather than who God says we are – and that never ends well. So, before you post, ask, 'Am I posting this to gain affirmation?'

Am I boasting?

Unless you are an out-of-control narcissist, you would never walk up to someone and say, 'Can I just tell you about how incredibly successful I am?' And yet, often our social feeds are screaming just that! But boasting is boasting whether it's in person or on Insta. So, before you post, check your motives and ask yourself, 'Am I just trying to make myself look good?'

Is it kind?

Social media is an easy place to vent. When we're filled with pent-up frustration, the easiest thing to do is pull our phones from our pockets and let it all out. But social media should not be a live feed of your inner monologue. The apostle Paul encourages us, 'Let your conversation be always full of grace' (Colossians 4.6), and we would do well to apply that same principle to our use of social media. So, never, ever post when you're angry – it's always a bad idea. Before venting online, pause for a minute and ask, 'Is it kind?'

*

Social media is a great tool if we use it right. So, apply these new rules to your digital world and you won't go far wrong. Happy posting!

Application questions

- Check your 'Screen Time' facility on your phone and see how much time you have spent on your phone over the last seven days. Now multiply this number by 52 to see how much of your year is given over to your phone. Are you happy with this number, or do you want to make some course adjustments?
- Of the 'new rules' suggested above, which do you feel would be beneficial to you? Can you begin applying them straight away?

PART 2
CULTURE AND
TEAM BUILDING

THE REAL POWER OF EFFECTIVE LEADERSHIP IS MAXIMIZING OTHER PEOPLE'S POTENTIAL.

BRIGADIER JIM WALLACE[1]

INTRODUCTION
'A GENIUS WITH A THOUSAND HELPERS'

———

'Tim, you're more of a Harley-Davidson than a bus.'

I liked the sound of that. I was sitting down over coffee with a leadership consultant, receiving some coaching, reflecting on my leadership together for a few hours. She said many things that were useful at the time, most of which I have since forgotten, but this particular comment will live with me for ever. I liked where this was going. Or so I thought, until she elaborated . . .

'You go really far, really fast, but you don't take many people with you.'

Ouch.

The real problem was she was right. I was making things happen, but largely on my own. I was making progress, but who was going with me? I had confused *achievement* with *leadership*. And they are not the same thing. Achievement is about what you are able to get done, leadership is about what you are able to inspire others to become. As Brigadier Jim Wallace, the former head of the Australian Special Forces, said, 'The real power of effective leadership is maximizing other people's potential.'

My leadership changed that day. I understood my calling in a new way and made immediate adjustments to my practice. I vowed to go a bit slower with a lot more people. I decided my leadership would be more about *who* I could elevate than *what* I could accomplish.

True leadership is about leveraging whatever influence you have to release others into their God-given potential, rather than accumulating people you can deploy to get your vision accomplished. The latter is what Jim Collins calls 'a genius with a thousand helpers'.[2] They are gifted leaders who delegate tasks rather than responsibilities. They recruit followers but fail to raise up leaders. Mike Breen, who leads the 3DM movement, expands on this idea in *Multiplying Missional Leaders*:

> We have one guy with a vision and a culture of volunteerism to help that one guy get his vision accomplished. He's the genius with a thousand helpers. So while churches may claim to have leadership development programmes, what they really have are volunteer pipelines. People go from being spectators to volunteers to managers as they get more involved, but they never become missional leaders.[3]

And that's why Part 2 of this book is all about building teams and creating cultures in which leaders can thrive *and* visions can become reality. It's about some of the things I've been learning in my attempt to become a little less like a Harley and a little more like a bus.

THE LANGUAGE THAT WE USE ESTABLISHES THE CULTURE WE CREATE.

11
CULTURE CLUB

One of the great privileges of my job is that I get to travel around and visit many different churches, youth groups, para-church organizations, festivals and events. The good news is, there is wonderful diversity in the Church. Nowhere else would you find such an eclectic mix of ages, cultures, nationalities and social groups united under one banner. The Church is a beautiful thing! Yet, among all this diversity, they all hold something in common: they all have a *culture*. Your church has a culture. Your youth or children's group has a culture. Your team has a culture. Even your meetings have a culture. You may not be able to articulate it but, make no mistake, your ministry has a culture.

Your culture is a set of (often unwritten) rules and values that determine behaviour within your ministry. Here's how some far more intelligent people than me define it:

> Culture is 'the sum-total of the learned patterns of thought and behaviour' of any given group.
> (Peter Scazzero)[1]

> [Culture is the] group norms of behaviour and the underlying shared values that help keep those norms in place.
> (John Jotter)[2]

> From the anthropological perspective, culture is the 'beliefs, customs, arts, etc., of a particular society, group, place or time'. From the business perspective, culture is 'a way of thinking, behaving or working that exists in a place or organisation'.
> (Liz Wiseman)[3]

Culture is the set of default behaviours and usually unexamined or unreflective practices that make uptake organisational life and ethos of a company, organisation, family or church. In short, organisational culture is 'the way we do things around here.'
(Tod Bolsinger)[4]

A healthy culture in your youth or children's ministry looks like a team who clearly understands the mission and vision of the team and are journeying with passion together towards that destination. It looks like leaders who know how to disagree in love because they are far too passionate about the mission of the team to waste time getting offended. It looks like everyone's opinions being valued, but no one holding their own ideas too tightly. It looks like mission being more important than the method, because there is no such thing as a sacred cow. It looks like clarity. It looks like alignment. And it's an environment in which team members and young people flourish.

How, then, do we establish that kind of healthy, fruitful culture within our children's and youth ministries? I agree with leadership expert Dr Henry Cloud, who said, 'What you create, [and] what you allow, is what you get as a leader.'[5] Spot on. Our culture is always a combination of what we create and what we allow. With that as our foundation, here are four keys to establishing a healthy culture.

1 Name it

If as a leader you haven't explicitly named the culture of your ministry, it doesn't mean that it hasn't got one; it means it has an *accidental* one. An accidental culture is one that has evolved organically according to the behaviours of the most influential characters in the group. When Jesus spoke of 'the yeast of the Pharisees' (Matthew

16.6), he was describing how the behaviours of a small group of influential individuals will quickly permeate an entire culture, though it doesn't necessarily serve the good of the group. How do we combat this? By creating a shared language.

Here's a leadership principle you'll want to take hold of: *the language that we use establishes the culture we create.* Mike Breen expounds upon this principle perfectly:

> whenever you talk about creating culture, you've got to start with language. You may have heard the saying that 'language creates culture,' and it's true. What you say, how you say it, and the mediums you use to say it will create a certain kind of culture. The problem for most of us is that we have a language people are using, but it's by accident. We need to approach culture-making with serious intentionality, allowing a shared language and vocabulary to create the culture God is calling us to shape.[6]

The language that we use establishes the culture we create, so if you want a healthy culture, you have to name it, write it down and talk about it again and again until you're blue in the face.

The primary means by which we begin to create this shared language is by clearly establishing the *core values* that permeate our ministries – a process to which we will dedicate the whole of the next chapter.

2 Model it

Once you have named the culture, the people you lead must now be able to look to you to see an example of what that culture looks like. So let's say you've named a culture in your team for everyone to arrive on time for every session. Guess what you need to do? Or perhaps you're seeking to build a culture of passionate worshippers among your young people. Guess what you need to be?

Leaders must never expect from others anything more than they're willing to live up to themselves. They should demonstrate in their own lives the same levels of commitment, diligence, passion and patience that they expect from those they lead. They offer themselves as an example to follow.

3 Challenge it

I'm willing to wager that this will be the first Christian publication in history that will encourage you to be intolerant! But if you wish to establish a healthy culture, intolerant you must be. Not of individuals, of course, but of behaviours that conflict with the culture you are creating. Patrick Lencioni writes: 'Great cultures tend to be appropriately intolerant of certain behaviours . . . After all, if an organization is tolerant of everything, it will stand for nothing.'[7]

Some time ago I was part of a team who were about to launch a new youth group in my home town. We had previously launched a group for 15–18-year-olds and were about to embark upon a second venture for 11–14-year-olds. We had already decided that we would set a culture of respect where no one talks and everyone listens to whoever is leading the session content. So before our first session I took a moment to remind our team to be intentionally intolerant of any behaviour that would subvert that culture by quickly challenging any young person who was talking when they should have been listening – and they did so magnificently! The culture was set and has been strong ever since.

Remember, your culture is a combination of what you create and what you allow; therefore, do not tolerate any behaviours that contradict your named culture, because, if you do, those behaviours will become the culture.[8]

4 Celebrate it

As much as we should confront behaviours that subvert the culture, we should celebrate those that affirm it. Executive Advisor Liz Wiseman writes: 'To build a strong culture, define the core beliefs . . . and ensure those beliefs are validated more frequently than they are violated.'[9] I agree with Wiseman on this. The frequency with which culturally congruent behaviours are validated is significant. Therefore, never miss an opportunity to celebrate someone who did something in line with the culture you are building – and wherever possible, do so publicly. If others in your group or team see you celebrating a certain behaviour, they are more likely to replicate it themselves. As Andy Stanley says, 'What's celebrated is repeated. The behaviours that are celebrated are repeated. The decisions that are celebrated are repeated. The values that are celebrated are repeated.'[10]

*

So here's what we do. We name the culture, we model the culture, we challenge any behaviours that do not reflect that culture, and we celebrate those that do. Do these four things and you will have a healthy culture in which your children, young people and team will thrive.

Application questions
- Write down one sentence that describes the current culture of your children's or youth ministry. (This could describe something positive or negative.)

- In one sentence, write down the aspirational culture of your children's or youth ministry.
- If your answer to these two questions is different, what steps might you need to put in place to move from your current culture to your aspired culture?

DEFINING OUR CORE VALUES IS REALLY THE PROCESS OF COMING INTO CLARITY ABOUT WHO GOD HAS ALREADY APPOINTED US TO BE AS A MINISTRY.

12

THE VALUE
OF VALUES

Identity formation. All of us in youth and children's ministry recognize the fact that one of the most important things we do is journey with our young people as they form their identity. This process of self-discovery is paramount for understanding who God has made them to be and what he has called them to do. There is something within all of us that understands, *you cannot fulfil your God-given potential until you understand your God-given identity.*

We recognize this to be true of the children and young people we journey with. We know this to be an indispensable part of our own personal discipleship and leadership development. Yet we often fail to recognize that the same is true of the ministries we lead. Understanding who we are as a ministry is a necessary prelude to stepping fully into the purposes God has assigned to us. Our ministries cannot fulfil their God-given potential until they understand their God-given identity. This, then, is the purpose of coming to clarity around our core values.

Your values define who you are. They are your identity, your character, your unique personality as a ministry. And coming into clarity around them is essential if you are to step into all the things that God has assigned to you.

That being the case, how do we come to clarify our values? Organizational health expert Patrick Lencioni can help us here. In his phenomenal book,

The Advantage, Lencioni helps us to understand what we are seeking to define and, first, what we need to avoid.

Aspirational values. 'These are the characteristics that an organization wants to have, wishes it already had, and believes it must develop in order to maximize its success.'[1]

Aspiring to something is no bad thing, of course, but aspiration is not what we're searching for here. Indeed, the very fact that you are aspiring to something demonstrates in itself that it is not a foundational part of your core identity; if you have to go after it, it's not already part of who you are.

Accidental values. 'These values are the traits that are evident in an organization but have come about unintentionally and don't necessarily serve the good of the organization.'[2]

This is the stuff we talked about in the previous chapter, where the behaviours of a small group of influential individuals can quickly permeate the entire culture of your team, group or ministry. It has to be addressed in order to be challenged, but the culture that has arisen accidentally is rarely something to be celebrated or affirmed.

Permission-to-play values. 'These values are the minimum behavioural standards that are required in an organization. Although they are extremely important, permission-to-play values don't serve to clearly define or differentiate an organization from others. Values that commonly fit into this category include honesty, integrity, and respect for others.'[3]

In our context as leaders of Christian youth and children's ministries, permission-to-play values would be things like 'creating a safe and welcoming environment for children and young people', or 'leaders with a vibrant personal relationship with Jesus and a passion for passing on the gospel to the next generation'. They are absolutely paramount for youth and children's ministry – we shouldn't be doing what we do without them – but that is the case for every youth and children's ministry everywhere in the world. And this why they don't serve us here: they are important, but they are not what make us unique.

*

In the process of seeking to clarify our values, we must avoid falling into the all-too-common pitfall of naming aspirational, accidental or permission-to-play values, because they do not achieve the primary task of uncovering, naming, celebrating and establishing our *core identity* in the culture.

So what sorts of values are we seeking to define? Those which Lencioni calls 'core values'.

Core values. 'Core values lie at the heart of an organization's identity, they do not change over time, and must already exist. In other words, they cannot be contrived.'[4]

Which brings us full circle to where we began: identity formation. Defining our core values is really the process of coming into clarity about who God has already appointed us to be as a ministry. Therefore, the process of defining our core values is less about *creating something* and more about *discovering something.*

In my context at Limitless, this process has been an absolute world-changer. Defining our core values was the process of putting language to what was already there, deep within our ministry. It made tangible what was previously intangible and enabled us to describe who we are: 'Family is our heart; Service is our posture; Listening is our culture; Excellence and Opportunity is our pursuit; Fun is our spirit; Pioneering is our calling.'

This changed everything. Our staff, leadership team and events planning teams all found a new anchoring point. Our decisions, methodology, structures, personnel are all held to account according to this unique identity. Discovering and putting language to these values has been a gift to me and a gift to our team. I'd even go as far as to suggest it's the single most important thing we have ever done for the health of our ministry.

Coming to clarity and alignment around your values will be transformative for your ministry and the people you lead. So why not take your team through this workshop and see what you discover?

Application questions: Core values team workshop

- Step 1: Take some time to explain clearly to your team the difference between aspirational, accidental, permission-to-play and core values.[5]
- Step 2: Print out the core values from a broad range of different organizations (include churches, Christian ministries, businesses, military, social sector organizations, and so on) and stick them up around the room. Ask your team to go around in pairs and discuss each one.
- Step 3: Come back together and ask the team to throw out ideas for what your core values might be. Write them all up on a flip chart. There are no bad ideas at this stage.

- Step 4: Highlight a maximum of six suggestions that most commonly resonate throughout the team. Then ask everyone in the room to independently write a sentence on each one.
- Step 5: Following the meeting, collate the ideas of the group into a set of (a maximum of six) values, and write a paragraph describing each one using the language of the team. In doing this you will create ownership, which is vital for keeping these values front and centre going forward.

I AM CONVINCED OF THIS: LEADERSHIP AT ITS VERY BEST LOOKS MUCH MORE LIKE FAMILY THAN HIERARCHY.

13
CREATING COMMUNITY

Joe was in Year 8 and had been part of our youth group, Limitless Malvern, for about 18 months. He has always been very intelligent and extremely articulate, consistently adding value to our conversations, which on this particular occasion were on the theme of influence. We had asked the young people to consider, 'Who are, or have been, the three most influential people in your life?'

Joe began to explain how his mum and his brother have had a significant impact on him, before adding, 'and the third one is a bit of a cheat answer, because it's not one person, it's my Limitless family'. I had a tear in my eye.

What might appear on the surface to be little more than a nice moment, I would go so far as to describe as one of the most moving moments in my youth ministry to date. Why? Because one of the things I intentionally pursue hard as a leader is creating a sense of community among those I am privileged to lead both locally and nationally, and this was one of those special occasions where it felt like the hard work was paying off.

I believe that so much of leadership is about creating community and engendering a sense of 'we're in this together', because when a community of people are in it together great things can happen. I am convinced of this: leadership at its very best looks much more like family than hierarchy.

Following one Limitless youth event, I was massively encouraged by some of the comments young people left on our Instagram post, asking what they enjoyed most:

'Just being surrounded by family.'

'Being surrounded by a massive family all worshipping together.'

'Our guys felt so much part of a family this time.'

'It was just such an amazing atmosphere, so proud to be part of this amazing Limitless family.'

And following our Limitless Leaders event for youth and children's ministry leaders:

'I had an amazing time with my Limitless family.'

'I love being part of Limitless, my heart is full.'

'For me, Limitless is like coming home.'

'Limitless is a place where I feel like I am accepted and that we are all family coming together.'

'I love Limitless because it's family, we have fun, and everyone is valued.'

I share these comments to demonstrate that community doesn't just happen, but neither is it restricted to geography. Community is much more about common purpose than common location.

In a world that is seemingly more entrenched and divided than ever, imagine what might happen if people could look at the Church and see a demonstration of unity across cultures, ethnicities, genders and generations. This kind of community is so deeply counter-cultural that I can't help but wonder, what if our most powerful witness is to demonstrate what it means to be *one*? We have to be a church that is deeply committed to loving each other before we can be committed to changing the world. So how do we create radical community among those we lead?

Common purpose

The starting place for any community bond is a clear and common purpose. Tod Bolsinger writes: 'Leadership is *always relational*. It is focused on a *community* of people who exist to accomplish a *shared* mission.'[1] Clarity of purpose is a gift to a community of people, because it acts as an anchoring point to an otherwise disparate group.

Think of a Premier League football team – this group of people couldn't be more different. They are multinational, multi-ethnic and multilingual, and yet when they step out on to the pitch they work together in perfect unity. Why? They have absolute clarity about their shared objective; they have come together to win the game. The principle we see at work here is this: *shared purpose is a far more powerful adhesive than shared interest.*

Intentional language

As we noted in our discussion on creating healthy culture, the language we use establishes the culture we create. Thus, if you want to have a group that feels like family, you must first talk about the group using the language of family. The quotes I shared above were not manufactured, but they are reflective of the sort of language our team has been using for years. Phrases like 'Limitless family' and 'family is our heart', along with words like 'together', 'unity' and 'community', are commonplace in our lexicon and, over time, that language has shaped our culture.

So mind your language! In your communication always use the language of 'we' and 'us', rather than 'you' and 'them'. The words, phrases and axioms we use, intentionally or otherwise, will play a significant role in shaping the culture of our communities.

Valuing people

With that said, you can't use this kind of community language if you don't really mean it! That's just leadership spin, and people (especially young people) will see through that artifice from miles away. Leadership that develops community requires that you genuinely care about those you lead. It requires that you care more about what God is doing through them than what they can do for you. Only when people believe that you are for them, not expecting them to be for you, will you begin to see authentic community being formed.

Authentic listening

Part of valuing people is about listening deeply and acting on what you hear. The nature of groups means being intentional about creating spaces to hear the voices of those you lead through sessions, Q&As, feedback forms, surveys, one-to-ones and so on. But this only helps to create community when the people you have taken the time to listen to can see their thoughts and ideas shaping the community of which they are a part. For example, at Limitless we have never had an event where the feedback we have received hasn't had an impact on the delivery of that same event the following year. We must listen authentically and respond with integrity to those we lead.

Loving communities fuelled by a common purpose have always been the way that God has chosen to change the world. In words often attributed to Margaret Mead, 'Never doubt that a small group of committed citizens can change the world. Indeed, it is the only thing that ever has.' And so we must take seriously the leadership responsibility of creating community, because battles are not won by heroes but by armies!

Application questions

- What are the deliberate words and phrases you are using to develop community? How can you help your team, children and young people speak that same language?
- In what ways could you enable your teams, children and young people to shape your activities this week?

IT IS IN THE GAP BETWEEN A PROBLEM ARISING AND THE PROBLEM BEING ADDRESSED THAT YOUR CULTURE IS ESTABLISHED.

14

SHOOT THE
ELEPHANT

I don't know about you, but I'm not a huge fan of confrontation. My natural inclination would be to run away from a potential conflict rather than towards one. Perhaps it's because of insecurity, perhaps it's because I don't like upsetting people, or perhaps it's because I want people to like me! Whatever it is, my default would be to let a problem go and hope that it will resolve itself rather than to bring it up and address it.

Unfortunately for me, I have come to understand that this is poor – even dangerous – leadership. Thus, one of the primary leadership lessons I have had to learn (and am still learning) is how to engage in healthy conflict.

So let me ask you a question: what are the problems in your youth or children's ministry that everyone knows are there but no one is talking about? These things are called 'the elephant in the room'. It's a problem, everyone knows it, but no one is addressing it. And here's the bad news: as the leader, it is your responsibility to shoot the elephant. And what's more, the time that elapses between an issue arising and it being addressed is hugely significant, because it is in the gap that your culture is established.

When we pioneered a new youth group in Malvern, we decided from the outset that, because we were going to be starting from scratch and thus working largely with non-Christians, we needed to set a strong culture up front, keeping in mind what we wanted the club eventually to become. Ultimately of course our prayer was that young people would come to faith, and that meant they needed to be hearing about Jesus. Our chosen means for this was a section within the night we called 'the Comfy Chair' (essentially a testimony slot with a jingle!), which would become the centre point of the club. It was absolutely crucial that the young people were fully attentive during this slot, and thankfully, because of some great work from the team and the goodness of God, it started off that way. However, after a couple of months, one of our regular young people brought a friend with her, and when it came to the Comfy Chair slot, and testimony was being shared, the new girl began chatting to her friend.

So what do you do in that situation? This girl was new; we were so glad she came and we wanted her to come back next week. With that in mind, would it be best to leave her to her conversation to ensure she had a great night? Or should it be confronted at the risk of offending her and putting her off from coming again? I know what I would lean towards, and I certainly know which is the easy option – but the easy thing and the best thing are very rarely the same thing. Here's what happened.

Almost immediately, one of our team who was sitting at their table leaned over and gently asked them to stop talking. They did, and she came back again next week. What's more, we never had an issue with that girl chatting during the Comfy Chair again. Why? Because it is in the gap between a problem arising and the problem being addressed that your culture is established. Our team member understood the culture we were trying to set, and because of the courage he showed in his willingness to confront the issue immediately, he protected and further established that culture.

There is a direct correlation between confrontation and culture. The level to which you are willing to confront issues is the level to which you establish and protect your culture.

This applies equally to your team. Sure, if you address an issue with a team member you have a chance of upsetting them, but leave it unaddressed and you have a chance of upsetting the entire team.

In the early days of our club, one of our team members, who is a fantastic leader and phenomenal youth worker, got into a habit of arriving a few minutes late to our team meetings. Everyone knew it, but no one was saying it. Elephant alert!

Now let's be fair, it wasn't really that bad, and perhaps if I had left it he would have started coming on time. But I knew that it is in the gap between a problem arising and the problem being addressed that your culture is established. Thus, had I allowed it to continue, I would have been unwittingly communicating to the whole team that in our culture it's OK to show up late. So I rallied myself, fought against my inner desire to avoid a confrontation and asked him for a chat. I explained that it was not OK to come late because that devalues the time of everyone who is sitting in the room waiting. I explained that we anticipated good punctuality, and that on the rare occasions where it is impossible to make it on time, an apology is made on arrival. And guess what? He very rarely came late again, and on the few occasions he did (as we all do from time to time), he was quick to apologize. Culture established.

So let me say it again. As the leader, it is your responsibility to shoot the elephant. Here's how.

How to shoot the elephant

Quickly. I've said it a few times already, but I'm going to say it again because it really is that important! *It is in the gap between a problem arising and the problem being addressed that your culture is established.* So don't delay that conversation you know you really need to have, don't leave it a month or a week, have it today!

Privately. Unless an issue has to do with your entire team or group, don't address it publicly. This will only humiliate the person you are confronting and is thus more likely to lead to a breakdown in relationship than a change in behaviour. Instead, sit with them one to one so that a meaningful conversation can take place. (And remember to keep your child protection protocol in mind if addressing a young person . . . but you already knew that!)

Gently. Confrontation doesn't have to mean conflict. This isn't a telling off. This isn't about you exerting authority. So think carefully about the tone of your voice and your use of body language. Be gentle and open-handed rather than aggressive and finger-pointing! It is possible to be both firm and gentle.

Candidly. That said, don't beat about the bush. If it's bad, say it's bad. Don't water down the issue because you're worried about upsetting the person, because if you do it's more likely to happen again.

Clearly. Be absolutely clear about what the problem is, be absolutely clear about what needs to change, and be absolutely clear about the consequences of repeated behaviour. I would even encourage you to make a mutually agreed-upon written record of the conversation to avoid any room for misunderstanding later on.

Graciously. Any confrontation, even if it includes some kind of discipline, must be restorative rather than punitive. Our heart in addressing the issue is not to put someone down or make them feel guilty; it is to see them fulfil their potential and become all they can be in God. So make sure there is always a pathway for restoration available.

Encouragingly. There may be an issue, but it's very unlikely that it's all bad. So this one-to-one is a great opportunity to encourage, build up and affirm the person you are talking to. Think before you meet about some of the wonderful qualities and contributions of this individual, and be sure they leave the meeting with those things ringing in their ears.

What if things go wrong?

Be warned, however, that even if you follow these steps to a T, there will still be occasions where your challenge is not well received. You could be met with defensiveness, even anger. So what do we do if things don't go to plan? Thankfully Jesus offers us some clear guidance here.

'If your brother or sister sins, go and point out their fault, just between the two of you. If they listen to you, you have won them over. But if they will not listen, take one or two others along, so that "every matter may be established by the testimony of two or three witnesses." If they still refuse to listen, tell it to the church; and if they refuse to listen even to the church, treat them as you would a pagan or a tax collector.' (Matthew 18.15–17)

Jesus gives us a really helpful step-by-step guide for confrontation that can be applied in our context as children's and youth ministry leaders:

1 We confront them individually.
2 We go with another team member.
3 We go with our church leaders.
4 If there's still no response, we step them down.

Perhaps that feels harsh to you, especially in a church context. Shouldn't we be exercising forgiveness? The answer to that, of course, is yes, absolutely! We are called to forgive again and again and again. But stepping someone down from our teams does not mean we haven't forgiven them; it means that we are being good stewards of the culture of the ministry that God has entrusted to us to lead.

Loving correction is one of the great, necessary challenges of leadership. So I pray that God gives you the courage and wisdom to graciously 'shoot the elephant'.

Application questions

- Are there any 'elephants in the room' in your ministry right now? What are they?
- Who do you need to talk to in order to shoot the elephant?
- Make a specific plan for engaging with the issue, utilizing the steps above.

THE PARADOX OF THE APOLOGY IS THIS: WHEN YOU OWN YOUR MISTAKES YOUR CREDIBILITY GOES *UP*.

15

THE PARADOX OF APOLOGY

———

It was about 10.30 p.m. when my phone buzzed with a text message from a colleague: 'Tim, we've got a problem . . .' We had stuffed up. Big time.

It was the eve of a national youth event with over 1,300 young people on their way to worship together. These events are an absolute monster to organize and cannot happen without a large team of hard-working volunteers who slog their guts out to serve the young people and leaders in attendance. Perhaps the greatest sacrifice for this team is that they commit to give up the comfort of their own beds, roll out a sleeping mat and spend a couple of nights 'sleeping' on a church floor.

Back to that text message:

> The volunteers arrived at their church accommodation but there was no one there. We called the pastor but they said nothing had been confirmed. He came down and let us in but it's not quite big enough for everyone. The guys and girls are in the same room.

It went on with some makeshift solutions that had been found, but this was bad. We had dropped the ball, we had messed up, and the volunteers were (understandably) upset. That night I couldn't sleep. I was devastated that we had let our volunteers down and was determined to make it right. And there was only one way that was going to happen.

The next morning I arrived early to ensure I was there to welcome the volunteers and join them in their team meeting (which I wasn't originally going to be attending). Some looked tired, some looked angry; all of them certainly had the right to be. So I stood up and did the only thing I could do:

'Guys, I heard about what happened with your accommodation last night and I want you to know that I'm sorry. That was not our plan, it was not our intention, and we have not honoured you here. It is my fault, it is not OK, there are no excuses, and I am sorry. We are going to sort this out for tonight, but until then we cannot do this event without you, so I'm asking that you would hear my apology, forgive us, and bring your best to God and to the young people today.'

And then something strange happened . . .

Applause.

Yes, you read that right, an actual round of applause. From everyone. The tension was lifted, the posture of the team changed, and that was that. We left it there, and the team smashed it that day.

And herein lies the paradox of an apology. We fear that publicly admitting and taking ownership for our mistakes will mean we lose the respect of our teams and young people. We worry that it will equate to broadcasting our incompetence such that onlookers lose their trust in our leadership. But the opposite is true. When something goes wrong, people are looking for the leader who will take responsibility for it. That is the leader they will respect. That is the leader they will trust. That is the leader they will follow. The paradox of the apology is this: when you own your mistakes your credibility goes *up*.

The paradox of apology

There's one more element to the story that it's worth taking a moment to reflect on. Practically I didn't actually have anything to do with organizing the accommodation. That wasn't my job, *but that didn't mean it wasn't my fault.* I was the leader, so ultimately the buck stopped with me.

If you are the leader then it is on you to take responsibility for the mistakes of your team. Yes, those mistakes can and should be addressed with your team members in private, but never, ever pass the buck on to another member of your team publicly. Whenever a leader shifts the blame in this way – someone else stuffed up, someone else made a mistake, someone else dropped the ball – their credibility is eroded.

In contrast, admitting your mistakes says something profound about your quality as a leader. It says something about your character; about your integrity. It shows people that you are trustworthy, that they can follow you and know they are not going to get publicly burned. The American businessman Arnold H. Glasow offers a principle that every leader should commit to memory: 'A good leader takes a little more than their share of the blame, and a little less than their share of the credit.'

Sometimes as leaders we can feel the pressure to be perfect and get everything right. The bad news is, we aren't and we don't! The good news is, people are looking for an authentic leader, not a perfect one.

So we are faced with a choice. Either we cover up and pass the blame for our mistakes, or we come right out and own it. And you will find that, when you do, your leadership credibility skyrockets. This is the paradox of apology.

Application questions

- Are you quick to front up for your mistakes, or do you always try and present your competence? What might be behind your reticence to apologize?
- Is there anyone to whom you need to apologize today? Why not put down this book and pick up your phone and make that call or send that message?

MAKE NO MISTAKE, BUILDING CULTURALLY, ETHNICALLY AND GENDER DIVERSE TEAMS IS NOT ABOUT TOKENISM, IT'S ABOUT ENSURING THAT YOU HAVE THE PERSPECTIVES YOU NEED TO MAKE ROBUST LEADERSHIP DECISIONS.

16
BUILDING DIVERSE LEADERSHIP TEAMS

———

Have you ever had a conversation that completely changed the way you lead?

As I reflect back over the last five years, I can think of just two occasions where I've had a conversation that was so significant my leadership changed in that very moment. I've shared the first one with you already (remember the Harley and the bus?). The second one was about lasagne.

Several years ago I was leading a summer festival event. We were drawing towards the end of the week when I crossed paths in the car park with Jordan, a youth leader from a large inner-city church who had been attending the camp with his young people. We got to chatting about the event, so I asked for his feedback. Jordan reflected that his young people had encountered Jesus and had a brilliant time, 'But there's just one thing,' Jordan added (and I quote), 'black kids don't eat lasagne.'

He went on to explain how our menu had not adequately catered for the tastes of his black-majority group; 'not enough flavour, more spice,' he explained. And while we did change the menu the following year, it wasn't the jerk chicken (though delicious!) that changed my leadership for ever. Because, although on the surface that conversation was about food, it revealed a significant leadership blind spot that I was unaware of until that moment.

The real problem wasn't the menu, the real problem was that I didn't have anyone on my team who would notice there was a problem with the menu. The real problem was that my team had too many people who looked like me and thought like me. The real problem was that my team lacked diversity and representation, and because of this *my team lacked perspective.*

When your team is full of people like you – who look like you, talk like you, think like you, or share the same gender, ethnicity or cultural background as you – your team is deficient because it lacks the perspective of the people who are not represented there. As a result you may be approving ideas or delivering sessions or casting visions that do not resonate with and will not engage the people who are not represented on your team.

We'd do well to remember that Scripture models this kind of diversity within leadership teams, as author and activist Ben Lindsay demonstrates:

> The Bible is a firm advocate of church leadership that reflects the community it serves. One of the best examples of diverse leadership in the Bible is Acts 13:1, with the leadership team in Antioch. This church leadership team was wonderfully heterogenous. The team comprised of Barnabas from Cyprus and a black man called Simeon . . . There was Lucius, who was possibly black as he was from Cyrene/North Africa. The team also included Manean, who was raised among royalty, and, finally, Paul, a Jew . . . The multicultural, multi-ethnic, multinational population of Antioch was reflected in the Church and in the

leadership. A mix of different backgrounds, different skills and gifts was a true reflection of the environment.[1]

What is true in Scripture in terms of ethnicity can equally be said of gender. I think of Junia, who was 'outstanding among the apostles' (Romans 16.7), the most senior level of leadership in the early Church. I think also of Priscilla who, alongside her husband Aquilla, led a church from her home in Corinth. Then there's Mary who sat at Jesus' feet, assuming the posture of a disciple, something that was unthinkable in a patriarchal society but lovingly affirmed by Jesus (Luke 10.42). Speaking of Jesus, would his ministry have even been possible without the 'many' women on his team who 'were helping to support them out of their own means' (Luke 8.1–3)? Or perhaps we should wind back the clock further still and consider Deborah, who 'was leading Israel at that time' (Judges 4.4). I could go on.

And so my spirit and my experience resonate with the truth of this statement from research professor Brené Brown: 'Only when diverse perspectives are included, respected, and valued can we start to get a full picture of the world.'[2] Make no mistake, building culturally, ethnically and gender diverse teams is not about tokenism, it's about ensuring that you have the perspectives you need to make robust leadership decisions.

You see, the lasagne conversation changed my leadership from that moment, because the way I constructed my teams changed from that moment. No longer was I only looking for people who had a high level of skill, a great amount of experience, or even a solid spiritual maturity. Now I was looking for people who had all of those things *and* were different from me and the other people on the team. I was intentionally on the lookout for people who would see things from a different point of view, from a different perspective and from a different cultural background. I was seeking team members who could represent young people who would experience our ministry in a different way than I experience it. And I cannot tell you how much richer our team, our ministry and my leadership is for it.

I have loved the learning that has been afforded to me by these leaders. I am refreshed by how they have opened my eyes to different perspectives. And I am grateful for how they have helped to shape our events and ministries in a way that makes them more engaging and accessible for people from all sorts of ethnicities and backgrounds. And while I am certainly no expert and am still very much on a learning journey with this stuff, one thing I can tell you is this: if you want a strong team, you need diversity.

We would do well to remember that the picture of heaven in the book of Revelation is of a great multitude from every nation, tribe, people and language (Revelation 7.9). Our purpose as the people of God is less about getting to heaven and more about getting heaven here. So let's build ministries that engage people from every tribe, by ensuring that our teams represent the different perspectives they need to thrive.

Application questions
- Spend a moment taking an audit of your team. Are they all similar to you? Do they share the same gender and/or ethnicity?
- Do the people in your team represent the children/young people in your ministry?
- What might you need to do in order to build a team that offers a broad range of perspectives in your context?

PERHAPS YOUR MOST SIGNIFICANT CONTRIBUTION TO THE KINGDOM OF GOD WILL NOT BE SOMETHING YOU DO BUT SOMEONE YOU RAISE.

17

PAY IT FORWARD: RAISING LEADERS

On 20 December 2015, at the BBC Sports Personality of the Year ceremony, 9-year-old Bailey Matthews stood before a live audience of thousands and a television audience of millions to collect the Helen Rollason Award for outstanding achievement in the face of adversity. His accomplishment? Overcoming his cerebral palsy to complete his first triathlon. The closing stage of the race, during which Bailey twice fell and picked himself back up, was captured on a spectator's phone and quickly went viral, receiving more than 81 million views. Bailey, quite rightly, was heralded an inspiration.

Moved as I am by Bailey's phenomenal achievement, there is another hero in this story by whom I am equally moved – Bailey's dad, Jonathan Matthews. Jonathan was with Bailey on every step of his journey: the training, the preparation, through the race itself. Even as he stood on the platform that day in Belfast to collect his award, there was Jonathan Matthews, beaming with pride, cheering Bailey on, and embracing him in his moment of triumph. Not a dry eye in the house!

Jonathan is a hero to me because he demonstrates the leadership principle that is shaping Part 2 of this book: leadership is not about what you are able to get done, but what you are able to inspire others to become. In short, leadership is fundamentally about *others*.

Justice advocate Danielle Strickland reminds us that 'great leaders use power to empower other people'.[1] With that in mind, all of us in a leadership capacity would do well to consider how we are getting on with releasing others into their God-given potential. Are we identifying leadership in others and creating opportunities for them to grow?

Identifying leaders

So what are the characteristics we should be noticing as we seek to identify leadership in our children, young people or volunteer team? Personally, I'm on the lookout for these three things.

1 Servant heart

The primary thing I'm seeking in emerging leaders is a willingness to serve without being asked and, crucially, without being given a title. I'm looking for those young people who are showing up early to set up and staying back late to pack down. I've got my eyes open for the team members who are the first to put their hands up (not the first to put their heads down) when there's a job that needs to get done.

The people who are willing to serve in the background are the ones to entrust with opportunity in the foreground. Conversely, beware the person who will only volunteer for the roles that get them on stage. These people are likely to be ambitious for themselves but not for the mission of the team – and let that be a red flag! As we know, Jesus came to serve not to be served (Matthew 20.28). He demonstrates to us the principle of servant leadership, and *all* Christian leadership must follow in his example. So follow the kingdom principle of the parable of the talents; find those people who are faithful in the small things and entrust them with something more.

2 Initiative

Often overlooked, but undoubtedly indispensable to leadership, is a good dollop of initiative. This is the difference between those two wonderfully servant-hearted young people who show up early to help you set up. The first young person shows up with a willingness to serve, but stands around twiddling their thumbs until someone gives them a job to do. The second is able to identify the jobs that need doing and crack on with getting them done. Their character is equally glorifying to God, but the second young person has leadership, the first does not.

Leaders act, leaders function, leaders *do*. Leaders take hold of the reins of life and make change happen. When identifying leadership in others you're looking for the seeds of these qualities evidenced through initiative.

3 Gifting

I remember the occasion we held a 'Bake Off' games night at our youth group in Malvern. As the young people moved around the different games stations, I couldn't help but notice how one young person would have an idea and, without a hint of bossiness, rally the people in her group to work on that idea together. That's leadership in its purest form, and it was my great joy to encourage her to that end when the session closed.

The apostle Paul writes to his mentee Timothy, 'fan into flame the gift of God that is *within you*' (2 Timothy 1.6, ISV). Leadership is a gift from God; it is *already within* some of the young people and team you lead, and will therefore reveal itself in moments like that. It's your job to be alert and name it when you see it.

Once we've identified leadership in the people around us, the next step is to raise them up.

Raising leaders

Model it

If you've been paying attention so far, the principle of 'modelling it' might seem familiar. This is the third time we've returned to it, for which I make no apology. That's because the most effective training for young leaders in not what you tell them, it's what you show them. The best learning is caught not taught. So let the leaders you are raising up see how you lead team meetings. Allow them to watch how you call out unhelpful behaviours, how you encourage your team, how you cast vision, how you work hard and how you pray hard. When you do this you'll begin to see the leaders you're investing in adopting leadership principles from you almost unconsciously, by osmosis.

Opportunity

If you delegate *tasks* you create followers, but delegate *responsibility* and you create leaders. Raising leaders, then, is much more about the opportunities we give than the words we say. But guess what? In order to create opportunities for others you have to move out of the way! Are there some things you're doing in your youth or children's ministry that someone on your team could benefit from giving a go?

I know that I wouldn't be doing what I'm doing today were it not for the leaders who entrusted opportunity to me. When I was 25 years old I was invited by my senior pastor to be an elder of a large city church. I'm sure there were many eyebrows raised in the congregation at the thought of a 25-year-old 'elder', but it was this opportunity that enabled me to see leadership potential in myself. So who are the young people within whom you see leadership, who may not yet see it in themselves? Perhaps the opportunity you entrust them with will be the catalyst that propels them into their calling. Be a springboard for your team to launch off, not a ceiling they can't break through.

Stretch, don't break

There is a fine line to tread when releasing opportunity to upcoming leaders. On the one hand, you want to give them something that feels beyond them – something that will cause them to work hard, pray hard and stretch their capacity to the next level. As Mike Breen says, 'Capacity can increase, but it will generally never increase until you reach the end of your current capacity.'[2] That's completely accurate but, on the flip side, push an emerging leader too far beyond their current capacity and you could be setting them up to fail, which would be a demoralizing setback in that person's leadership journey. So try to find opportunities that will stretch, but not break, the leaders you're developing.

Evaluate and encourage

Commit to continually reflecting with your young leaders on their practice. Never let them do something well without pointing it out. Remember, 'what's celebrated is repeated'. So be specific in your encouragement. Not just, 'You did really well tonight', but, 'You did really well tonight *because . . .*' and fill in the blank. This kind of effusive, specific praise will stay with young leaders for a long time. It communicates that you believe in them, that you're proud of them, and makes them more receptive to the kind of challenge they need from you in order to grow.

Evaluate and challenge

In the context of encouragement, appropriate challenge is absolutely vital for growth. Don't shy away from conflict. Address issues quickly before they spiral out of control. Sometimes you'll need to address character issues; at other times your feedback will be more practical. Where possible try to stick to one thing to improve at a time. A long list of things to improve can be overwhelming and highly demotivating.[3]

Journey

Unfortunately, you can't microwave a leader! These things take time. So be committed to journeying with emerging leaders over a number of years, entrusting them with bigger things as they demonstrate faithfulness in smaller things. Elisha travelled with Elijah for seven years before he took up Elijah's mantle. Timothy travelled with Paul for 15 years before being entrusted with leadership of the church in Ephesus. Invite young leaders on a journey with you, and stay the course.

One of the greatest joys I have experienced in youth ministry to date came at the conclusion of a three-year leadership development journey. Following some conversations with local teenagers and a couple of weeks in the schools, a team of young leaders and I were nervously about to open the doors to a brand new youth group. Keren, just 18 at the time, was a member of that team whom we had asked to oversee our prayer space. She wasn't among our more experienced or even more naturally gifted leaders, but it quickly became apparent that she was among the most faithful, responsible and hungry to learn.

After an academic year of delivering on her responsibilities and giving her best every week, we asked her to lead a new discipleship small group on a Sunday morning to help connect the young people we were reaching through the youth ministry with the wider church. This was definitely a step up for her, but her hunger to learn saw her leadership gift multiplying in leaps and bounds. While initially stretched, she soon found the capacity to make it happen, and delivered a quality experience for our young people every week.

So, in year three, we asked Keren, now 20, to lead the whole team alongside me. Again she was stretched, encountering some leadership challenges she hadn't experienced before, but once again engaged with the opportunity head on. Month by month I took more of a back seat as she grew into her new role, finding the confidence and capacity to lead.

Which brings us to that moment of great joy, when, as that academic year drew to a close, the church elders, youth team and I stood together at the front of our local church and prayed for Keren as she took on full leadership of our youth ministry. It's now my great joy to be on her team and serve under her leadership!

Remember, leadership is not about what you are able to get done, but what you are able to inspire others to become. As former US President John Quincy Adams once said, 'If your actions inspire others to dream more, learn more, do more and become more, you are a leader.' So, let's have a radar for the potential in others, and seek to raise up and release leaders into their God-given calling. Perhaps your most significant contribution to the kingdom of God will not be something you do but someone you raise.

Application questions

- Who are the children, young people or team members in your sphere of influence who exhibit a servant heart, initiative and gifting? Write down their names and ask God if he is asking you to invest in them.
- Are there things you are currently doing that, if you passed them on, would give someone else an opportunity to grow?
- Are there areas in which you could give people a glimpse 'behind the scenes' of your leadership process?

IN UNSTOPPABLE TEAMS, EVERYONE KNOWS EXACTLY WHAT IS REQUIRED OF THEM.

18

HOW TO LEAD A VOLUNTEER TEAM

I love our young people; they are fun, courageous, tenacious, thoughtful, open-hearted, kind and authentic. I look forward to hanging out with them each week, and I have come to develop a deep affection for them. And I know you feel the same for your children and young people too! I know you got into this job and continue to give the best of yourself because you love them, believe in them, desire the best for them and long to see them fulfil their God-given potential.

But there is a group of people that you cannot do this without: your team of volunteers.

Volunteers are the true heroes of the Church and of youth and children's ministry in particular. The Church pours hundreds of thousands of volunteer hours into children and young people every year. Perhaps you are a volunteer at your local church yourself, as I am. Whatever your circumstances, volunteers are the engine that drives youth and children's ministry forward, and we cannot do it without them.

That being the case, can I ask you to consider, do you give as much thought to leading your team as you do to leading your young people? Do you consider their journey, their spiritual development, their well-being, their growth, in the way you do for your children and young people? Or is there a danger that your volunteers have become pawns you utilize to help you get the job done?

The truth is, you probably didn't get into kids' or youth work because you wanted to lead a team, but I want to make the case that you are equally responsible for leading the volunteers that God has entrusted to you as you are the children and young people. With that in mind, here are five of the best gifts you can give to your volunteer team.

1 The gift of direction

Your first responsibility as a team leader is to make sure everyone is aiming at the same target. Consider it this way: if you were to ask everyone on your volunteer team individually to write down the purpose of your children's or youth ministry, would they all write the same thing? If not, gather your team and have that discussion asap!

At Limitless Malvern, we are clear that we are all about 'helping those who are far from God discover full life through Jesus'. That means everyone on our team knows we don't exist only to disciple the Christian young people who already go to the church. We're not here to provide a hang-out space, or only to help young people navigate difficult challenges. We exist to help people who don't know Jesus find new life in him.

Your purpose may be very clear to you, but do your team know it and own it in the way you do?

2 The gift of clarity

The next stage is to ensure that every volunteer knows exactly what is expected of them personally. One of my favourite passages from Scripture is from the book of Joel in *The Message* paraphrase: 'The invaders charge. They climb barricades. Nothing stops them. Each soldier does what he's told, so disciplined, so determined. They don't get in each other's way. *Each one knows his job and does it.* Undaunted and fearless, unswerving, *unstoppable*' (Joel 2.7–11).

In unstoppable teams, everyone knows exactly what is required of them. That's why everyone on our team is given a specific role. Whether it's running registration, ice breakers, music, testimonies, the cafe, or whatever, each one knows their job and does it. We also have a clearly outlined expectation that 'everyone brings their best every time'. We don't want passengers on our team. We don't want one of the team members to have to do double the work because someone else can't be bothered. Maybe that sounds harsh, but the quickest way to demotivate a volunteer is to waste their time. Don't have people kicking their heels waiting for something to do. This unintentionally communicates to team members that they are surplus to requirements, and they won't last on the team for long.

3 The gift of responsibility

As we said in the chapter on raising leaders, if you delegate tasks you create followers, but delegate responsibility and you create leaders. When I was leading Limitless Malvern, I made it my goal to hand over as much of the leadership responsibility as possible, before I handed it over entirely. At one stage we had three weekly sessions – a Tuesday night outreach for two different age groups and a Sunday morning discipleship group – and I didn't lead any of them; I had three great volunteers who did that. I rarely led any of our team meetings; I had a fantastic volunteer who did that. I didn't host the testimony slot. You guessed it! Another brilliant volunteer.

Your team can't grow in your shadow. So where are the opportunities and responsibilities that you can be entrusting to your volunteers, according to their character and gifts?

4 The gift of encouragement

Encouragement is a recurring theme that runs throughout the 'Culture and team building' section of this book. That's because healthy teams and life-giving cultures thrive in an environment of encouragement. So here's a practical idea for you that I shamelessly stole from a church worship team after I visited as a guest speaker. It's called 'Shout outs'.

The idea is simple. After a session with your children and young people, gather your team and ask everyone to give a 'shout out' to another team member for something good they did in the session. The beauty of this idea is that, when people know this exercise is coming, they will be actively on the lookout during the session for the good things their team mates are doing in order to have something to say at the end. It's a practical way to ensure team members are continually validated and encouraged, and will begin to establish that culture of encouragement around your team.

5 The gift of feedback

Don't neglect the debrief. Help your volunteers to see the things they're doing brilliantly, as well as the things they need to improve on. This type of constructive feedback is absolutely vital for growth, which is why the next chapter is dedicated to just that.

You and I have a great gift: we get to invite our volunteers to be used by God in ways they never imagined. We are enabling them to experience the purpose and fulfilment that comes from participating in the cause of Christ. So, as much as you and I love our children and young people, let's take seriously our responsibility to lead the most dynamic, passionate, God-centred, life-giving teams possible.

Application questions

- Do your volunteers have clarity regarding the overall objectives of the team? Has this been defined in writing and do you repeat it regularly? If not, how could you help your team find clarity around your shared purpose?
- Does everyone on your team have a specific role and responsibility? If not, could you consider distributing the various responsibilities required to run your children's or youth ministry to different team members? Who in your team would thrive in which role?

WHEN WE SHY
AWAY FROM
OFFERING REGULAR,
THOUGHTFUL,
CONSTRUCTIVE
FEEDBACK, WE
ROB THE PEOPLE
WE LEAD OF THE
OPPORTUNITY
TO GROW.

19

THANKS FOR
THE FEEDBACK

Earlier in the 'Culture and team building' section of *Leadership 101*, I shared with you two bits of feedback that changed my leadership for ever. The first ('You're more of a Harley-Davidson than a bus') changed my entire perspective on leadership. I stopped trying to do things as fast as I could and started involving as many people as I could. I stepped away from opportunities I enjoyed in order to create more opportunities for the people that I lead. And all because of one piece of insightful, constructive feedback.

The second ('black kids don't eat lasagne') transformed my approach to building teams. I stopped looking only for skills and started looking for skills *and* perspectives, and my teams are far richer as a result. Just imagine, then, how comparatively deficient my leadership would be today had these two people not found the courage to say it as they saw it.

Here's the point: when we shy away from offering regular, thoughtful, constructive feedback, we rob the people we lead of the opportunity to grow. As such, the art of learning to give good feedback is a must for every leader who wants to draw out the potential in the people around them. And yet, giving feedback is an inherently delicate matter. The very essence of constructive feedback requires pointing out where people are *not* doing things well, and thus requires a considered approach. So how do we give helpful and effective feedback?

Build trust

A wise man once told me, 'Trust is the currency of change.'[1] He was right. Before you can expect your feedback to be well received, the person you are giving the feedback to must trust you in two ways. First, they must believe that you genuinely have their best interests and personal growth at heart. Second, they must believe that you know what you're talking about. In formulaic terms:

Demonstrated integrity (over time) + Demonstrated competency (over time) = Trust.

And much like Rome, trust isn't built in a day. Take time to get to know the people you lead. Take a genuine interest in their lives. Demonstrate your love and care for them. Then you will engender the kind of trust that will permit you to speak into their lives.

Create a culture of encouragement

As we've said already, *never let anyone do anything good without pointing it out*. Wherever you see a positive behaviour, an extra-mile effort or a demonstration of competency, celebrate it! Celebrate it publicly if you can. Point out how great it was in front of everybody. And be specific. Good feedback never starts with what needs to be improved, because continually being told what to do better is exhausting and demotivating. Good feedback thrives in a culture of encouragement.

Not just what, how

When the time comes to offer suggestions for change, be careful not only to point out *what* needs to change. Always ensure the 'what' is accompanied by a 'how'. We don't just say, 'You need to improve your youth talks.' We say, 'I think we could work a little on your talk introductions. Why don't you try opening with a funny story instead of going straight into the Bible passage next time?' See the difference? Feedback without follow-up is like telling someone to climb a mountain with no equipment. When we point out an area for improvement we must ensure we give people the tools they need to make that change.

Create a culture of accountability

Even when we've built trust, offered encouragement and suggested pathways for improvement, feedback can still be fruitless without this often forgotten principle: it is the leader's responsibility to hold the person to account for the changes they have agreed upon. Let's say you have a team member who always shows up late. You challenged them on their punctuality and have agreed steps forward. Then they show up late for the next session. Like a good leader, you pull them aside and challenge them. They apologize . . . and turn up late again next time. So you tell your friends, the other team members, your spouse, your boss – everyone but them! And I get that – no one likes to nag. But without continual, consistent accountability, ingrained behaviours are very unlikely to change. Giving feedback is just the start; accountability is where the real change happens.

Remember, when we fail to give feedback we rob those we lead of the opportunity to grow. For most of us, giving effective feedback isn't natural or comfortable, but it is essential. So apply these principles and help the people around you to flourish.

Application questions
- What are the best pieces of feedback you have ever

been given? What was it about how that feedback was communicated that helped you to grow?

- Who on your team would benefit and grow as a result of some feedback? Set aside some time to invest in their leadership development.

THE BEST MEETINGS HAPPEN WHEN EVERYONE IS FULLY ATTENTIVE AND ENGAGED, AND WHEN THE WHOLE TEAM FEELS THEIR CONTRIBUTIONS ARE VALUED.

20
HOW NOT TO HATE MEETINGS

Everyone hates meetings, right? They are the necessary evils we have to endure in order to get to the real work of investing in children and young people.

If you think that way, I can't blame you. We have all sat through meetings that seemed rudderless, straying from tangent to tangent according to the latest carriage on the next person's thought train. We've all had to endure those meetings that seemed to go nowhere and produce nothing. We've all sat with eyes glazed over as the chair of the meeting droned on and on about who knows what. We were at best bored and at worst downright angry at having our precious time wasted in another fruitless meeting when we've got more than enough to be getting on with, thank you very much!

But does it really have to be this way? Is it possible that meetings could be life-giving instead of soul-destroying? Could they become something we look forward to instead of something we dread? I believe they can.

Have you experienced it? The joy of a team on the same page, equally passionate about the mission God has entrusted to you, pursuing God's will together? The moment in the meeting when that lightbulb goes on, that realization hits, that fresh revelation comes? It's glorious! I really believe there is something unique about the way God speaks to a team that he doesn't with individuals, for surely God made us to journey together in community?

That's why I believe that, when they're done right, meetings don't have to be something we endure but something we enjoy, even look forward to. Imagine a meeting culture where we can't wait to gather with our friends, engage in the issues that matter, dream big dreams, pray big prayers, and make big decisions that will influence countless lives. Sounds good?

Whether or not you experience this, though, depends almost entirely on how your meetings are led. So here are my top ten tips for leading meetings that matter.

1 Prepare adequately

You can tell within two minutes whether the chair of a meeting has thought ahead to the purpose of the meeting, or if they have just shown up because it was in the diary. Before you lead your next meeting ensure you have internally answered this question: if we could only make one clear decision in this meeting, what would it be? Clearly answering this question gives you focus going into the meeting, enabling you to prioritize the most important issues and discuss them when everyone is fresh and alert.

Also ensure that you circulate your agenda to everyone in the team *before* arriving at the meeting, which gives people time to do some preparation and pre-thinking. Your team won't then have to process in the moment, which leads to clearer thinking, more articulate discussions and far less rambling in your meetings.

2 Land in action or alignment

Don't move on from your discussion until you have landed in decisive action or more clearly aligned thinking. This, more than anything else, will get rid of those meetings that were utterly pointless because nothing changed as a result. So make sure you always know who is doing what, by when, before you move on in the meeting. At the end of each item on the agenda take a moment to reflect on the decisions made to be sure that everyone in the room has heard and internalized the same thing.

3 Everyone take note of their own actions

Hopefully you'll have someone in the room taking minutes. This is good and important, but has a downside: people rely on the minutes to record *their* responsibilities. The problem with this is, let's face it, people don't read minutes! At the start of the meeting, ask everyone in the room to take note of their own action points. Then, before closing the meeting, go round the room and ask everyone to share what they have agreed to do from their record.

4 Ban phones

This may sound radical, but I've banned phones in my meetings. I do allow exceptions if people are expecting a very important call from home, but ask that they communicate this to the whole team at the start of the meeting. Why do I do this? Because no matter how accomplished a multi-tasker you are, if you're looking at your phone when someone else is speaking it communicates that you are not particularly interested in what they have to say. Whether you *are* interested or not is irrelevant. Whether you *can* look at your phone and be attentive at the same time is irrelevant. It's about what it communicates to the others in the room. The best meetings happen when everyone is fully attentive and engaged, and when the whole team feels their contributions are valued. As Netflix CMO Bozoma Saint John says, 'If people in your meetings are not being heard, they are not going to show up with their full selves.' Therefore, ensure everyone switches off so they can be switched on!

5 Keep to time

People are busy. They probably have another appointment scheduled for directly after your meeting. Honour their time by finishing on time, even if you haven't finished your agenda. If you keep running over, people will start to resent coming to your meetings, and that's not a good place to start.

Equally, start on time, even if you're still waiting for people to arrive. When you wait for everyone to show up before starting the meeting it communicates that it's OK to be late, and so that behaviour is easily repeated, whereas no one likes to walk into a meeting that's already started. It's embarrassing, and they are therefore less likely to be late again next time.

To help you stick to time I'd also recommend you break down how long you are going to spend on each item on the agenda before the meeting begins. If you don't do this, the time you are able to give the items at the end of your agenda will likely get squeezed, if not lost all together.

6 Encourage conflict

Wait, what? *Encourage* conflict? You mean *discourage* conflict, right? Wrong. One of the most important roles for the chair of a meeting is to ensure that everyone says it exactly as they see it, especially when they see it differently to the people who have already spoken. This kind of robust dialogue ensures that an issue is properly tested before it is given any airtime outside the room and stops 'the meeting after the meeting', when team members complain to each other about what was decided in the meeting! You need to learn to be comfortable with people disagreeing, because if your team are passionate they *should* have an opinion. As long as passionate disagreement takes place about an issue, not an individual, then this kind of conflict should be encouraged. Make sure your team know that in your meetings it is OK to disagree with each other and with you, but it's not OK to have a contrary opinion that you're keeping to yourself.

7 Don't require consensus

Encouraging healthy conflict eradicates the need for consensus in the room in order to move forward. To paraphrase Patrick Lencioni, most reasonable people don't need to get their own way all the time; they just need to know they've been heard. If you require a total consensus before moving forward, progress will be painfully slow and many great ideas will be shut down because of a couple of contrary voices. So ensure that you listen to your team, allow yourself to be persuaded by their arguments, take the temperature in the room, and then make a decision – even if it's not the decision everyone in the room wanted. As long as those in the meeting have been authentically listened to, they should be able to get on board and back the decision.

8 Defined purpose

It is very difficult for the human brain to switch between detail and creativity. So wherever possible try to keep creative meetings, financial meetings, reflective meetings and strategic meetings separate from each other or, at the very least, take a decent break – and even go to a different room – before switching gear.

9 Think environment

Is the environment conducive to the discussion? If the meeting is creative in nature, then sitting round a table with laptops in front of you is not likely to bring the best out of your team. If it is financial, then sitting around on armchairs with nowhere to place your budget papers is not particularly helpful either.

Space is also important. You want to create a level of intimacy without feeling squashed. If your team are sitting too far away from one another it becomes very easy to disengage, too close and people will feel uncomfortable, creating tension and hampering creativity. We all appreciate a bit of personal space.

Leadership expert Simon Sinek says, 'The role of the leader is not to come up with all the great ideas. The role of the leader is to create an environment in which great ideas can happen.'[1] So create an environment that helps to focus and bring the best out of the team *according to the core purpose* of that meeting.

10 Good tangent/bad tangent?

This is a tricky one. Tangents can make meetings frustrating and fruitless, where you bound from one idea to the next according to whatever pops up in people's minds at the time. This kind of meeting results in a lot of talking and very little progress. Yet, in my context at Limitless, some of the best ideas we've ever had were born of tangents. It is the role of the leader to discern two things. Is this tangent helpful or not? And, if yes, is this for now or is this for later? You can then steer the direction of the meeting accordingly. Don't be afraid, and jump in by saying, 'That's some good stuff, but today we need to come to a decision on this issue, so I've made a note of that and we'll return to it next time.'

*

Love them or loathe them, meetings are an inseparable part of your ministry journey. Done right they can be the chrysalis where your best, most creative, God-given ideas are born, shaped and nurtured. They can be the place where friendships grow deeper and camaraderie is fostered. A well-led meeting could just be the place where the next big idea is born; where God breathes new life and fresh vision into you and your team.

Application questions

- How do you feel about the meetings you attend/lead? What is it about these meetings that you love/hate?
- Of the ten top tips outlined above, which are you going to apply to your next team meeting?

PART 3
VISION AND
STRATEGY

'THE ROLE OF THE LEADER IS TO TAKE PEOPLE FROM WHERE THEY ARE TO WHERE THEY HAVE NEVER BEEN.'
JOHN GLASS

INTRODUCTION
GETTING FROM HERE TO THERE

———

It was one of the best meetings I've ever been in.

We were a couple of years away from the 100-year anniversary of the Elim Pentecostal Church, the movement of churches I belong to, and we were discussing with our team what we might do to help the young people in our churches mark this historic moment and launch into the next century. What could we do to celebrate a significant landmark without enshrining nostalgia?

The conversation was beginning to pick up momentum as ideas were bandied about. It felt as if we were on to something. The Holy Spirit was present. There was an electricity in the room.

Before long, pretty much the whole team were standing up. The tempo and volume of our conversation had ratcheted up a few notches. People were moving to and fro from the flip chart, writing stuff up, crossing stuff out, developing the burgeoning idea that was beginning to take shape. It was thrilling.

Before long the idea was landed: 100 gatherings, in 100 locations, over 100 days, to celebrate 100 years – all of which would culminate in a massive single get-together at the conclusion of the 100-day period. We had a vision; a measurable destination. We knew what we wanted to do and when it needed to get done, and we had a lot of fun imagining it.

The trouble is anyone can do that. Anyone can dream big dreams. Anyone can close their eyes and imagine a brighter future for their ministries. The vision bit is the fun bit. But if the role of the leader is to take people from where they are to where they have never been, they need more than a vision; they need a strategy.

Strategy is far less sexy than vision, but it's where the rubber hits the road. The ability to form and execute a clearly defined strategy is where vision becomes reality. And I can tell you that the meetings where we discussed how we were actually going to make 100 gatherings, in 100 locations, over 100 days happen were significantly less fun than the one where we dreamed up the idea! But the inconvenient truth is this: *in order to do the things we really want to do tomorrow, we have to do the things we really don't want to do today.*

Part 3 of this book is all about vision and strategy. It's about getting on God's agenda and following him wherever he leads. It's about dreaming audacious dreams and working to see those dreams become reality; about learning to bring clarity to our thinking and translate that thinking into actionable steps. It's about becoming leaders who dream about change, talk about change and make change happen.

A CLEARLY DEFINED MISSION HAS THE POWER TO BRING TO THE SURFACE OF YOUR LIFE, SCHEDULE AND PROGRAMME THE THINGS THAT MATTER MOST.

21
DEFINE YOUR MISSION

———

'What is the most important thing you have done in your ministry?'

It's a big question, isn't it? And an interesting one to reflect on. How would you answer it?

When I was asked this very question, it caused me to review the years in which I have had the privilege to lead the ministry of Limitless. I considered some mile-marker moments along the journey; significant initiatives that we had launched and events we had run. I reflected on new youth groups that had been pioneered in churches with no young people. I recounted the stories of changed lives, which are undoubtedly the 'why' behind the 'what' – the reason we do what we do. But as I considered these things it struck me that they were results, symptoms, if you like, of less visible things that had happened behind the scenes.

To lean into another metaphor, these things were like the fruit on the tree. But a tree doesn't bear fruit by tending to the fruit; rather, by tending to the root. The things that exist beneath the surface are the things that ultimately determine its fruitfulness.

'What is the most important thing you have done in your ministry?' That was the question. And it occurred to me that in the previous years there were three 'roots' that we had carefully attended to, to which the aforementioned fruitfulness could be directly traced.

'The most important thing I've done,' I replied to my friend, 'is to help our team come to absolute clarity around our mission, vision and values.'

Not very sexy, is it? And certainly not the reason you got into youth and children's ministry. But fruit is determined by the root. My encouragement to you, therefore, is that leading your team to clarity around your mission, vision and values could be one of the most important things you ever do as a leader, because it will directly result in a more fruitful youth or children's ministry.

We've already discussed 'The value of values' in the 'Culture and team building' section of this book. There we discussed how our values serve to define our personality – our core identity – as a ministry. But what about mission and vision? What are they, and how do they help shape our ministries?

Mission = what you do

Your mission is *what* you do. It defines what you will, and will not, give your time to. It creates a clear filter through which to pass all of your decision-making, the resources you will use, the events you will engage with, and the training materials you will utilize. Having a clearly defined mission has the power to bring to the surface of your life, schedule and programme the things that matter most.

At Limitless we have defined our mission – what we do – in this way: equipping leaders and inspiring churches to raise up a limitless generation.

It is impossible for me to overemphasize how helpful that simple sentence has been, because our mission has become the filter through which we pass all of our decision-making and activity. It has become the plumb line against which we measure success, the lighthouse that keeps us on course.

In his excellent book *Canoeing the Mountains*, author and pastor Tod Bolsinger expresses this thought powerfully:

> The mission trumps. Always. Every time. In every conflict. Not the Pastor. Not the members of the church who pay the bills. Not those who scream the loudest or who are in the most pain. No. In a healthy Christian ministry, the mission wins every argument. The focussed, shared, missional purpose of the church or organization will trump every other competing value.[1]

He goes on to say, 'There is perhaps no greater responsibility and no greater gift that leadership can give a group of people on a mission than to have the clearest, most defined mission possible.'[2]

I have found this to be true over and over again. Clearly defining our mission has served me when bringing new people into our teams, because they immediately know what they are signing up for, enabling them to hit the ground running. It has given clarity to decision-making in team meetings, and united us together by providing a shared purpose to rally around.

I remember when we went through this process with our local youth ministry. We gathered our team in my home and began to go through some exercises to help us come to clarity about our mission. After some robust dialogue and a bit of wordsmithing, we landed on this mission statement: 'Helping those who are far from God discover full life through Jesus.' And, as Tod Bolsinger promised, it was indeed a 'gift'. It gave us an anchoring point in terms of clarity and a springboard in terms of direction. Suddenly, like putting on a pair of prescription glasses for the first time, the intangible purpose we were seeking to grasp had become crystal clear. We knew what we were about. We were a team.

So, if it really is that important, how do you define your mission? I'd like to offer the following steps as a practical workshop you can lead your team through, to come to shared missional clarity.

Will you give this great gift to your team?

Application questions
Defining your mission: team workshop

- *Step 1.* Give your team an envelope with everything you do through your youth or children's ministry on individual pieces of paper inside.
- *Step 2.* Ask your team to consider: 'If our time and/or budget was cut by 50 per cent, which things would we fight to keep going and which would we have to stop?' Then ask your team to take each of the activities from the envelope and place them within three buckets, marked 'Yes', 'Maybe' and 'No', according to their importance under those circumstances.
- *Step 3.* Compare the results. Are there some things that the majority of the team put in the 'No' bucket? Is it time to stop those things? Are there some things that the majority of the team put in the 'Yes' bucket? What does that tell you about your priorities? Discuss these things together.
- *Step 4.* Having clarified your priorities, ask your team individually to write a one- or two-sentence mission statement that describes the purpose of your ministry. No consultation allowed!

- **Step 5.** Go round the room and ask your team to read out their mission statements. Write key words/phrases/ideas on a flip chart and highlight the priorities that are reflected by multiple team members.
- **Step 6.** Take that flip chart away and use it to craft a short, memorable mission statement based on the key priorities identified by the team.

VISION PAINTS A CLEAR PICTURE OF A GOD-ORDAINED FUTURE THAT MOBILIZES PEOPLE TO JOURNEY TOGETHER TOWARDS THAT DESTINATION.

22
VISION: FROM CONCEPT TO TARGET

_____

When was the last time you went to see a 3D movie? Did you remember to bring the glasses with you that you paid for last time? Of course you didn't! And when you got into the cinema with your brand new set of overpriced glasses, and the movie started playing, did you tip off your glasses to see what the picture looked like without them? Of course you did! And what was it like? It was fuzzy, right? The image was messy. Not easy to define. But when you popped those glasses back on, the image jumped back into life and clarity resumed.

Defining your mission, vision and values will do exactly that for your ministry: give you clarity and bring it to life. The decisions that once felt fuzzy will be made with a new clarity. The direction that once felt unknown will come with a new certainty, and the trajectory of your ministry will come to life.

Vision = where you are going

If values describe _who you are_, and your mission defines _what you do_, then your vision dictates _where you are going_. It is a clearly defined destination. A measurable goal. (Or, for those of you partial to a bit of alliteration, values are for producing a healthy culture, mission for providing a common purpose, and vision for proclaiming a clear direction!)

Vision paints a clear picture of a God-ordained future that mobilizes people to journey together towards that destination. It is the rallying cry that teams gather around, inspiring them to maintain consistent effort week after week, year after year. As Andy Stanley puts it, 'Vision is a clear mental picture of what could be, fuelled by the conviction that it should be.'[1] It's when you have a deep conviction that something has to happen, coupled with a clear idea of how to make it happen.

Without a clearly defined vision we are in danger of leading our teams around in circles, doing the same things over and over again just because they're the things we've always done, or doing the new things that seem to be working because they're what someone else has done. Leading without vision is what Jesus described as 'the blind leading the blind'. And do you remember how that worked out? I'll give you a clue . . . it wasn't good (Luke 6.39).

If you don't have vision you will get lost. That's one thing if you're out on your own, but another thing entirely if you are a leader and taking others with you. Thus, clearly defining and communicating vision is an outstanding priority for every leader, because, as American politician Aja Brown reminds us, 'People can't go with you if they don't know where you want to go.'[2]

So if vision is really that important, how do I get one?

How do I get a vision?
1 Holy discontent
Andy Stanley says, 'Visions are born in the soul of a man or woman who is consumed with the tension between what is and what could be.'[3] That being the case, the best place to start is with things that break your heart. What is happening in our society that you simply cannot tolerate? What patterns do you see in the lives of your children

and young people that you just can't stand? What is happening in your community that you just have to see change? These areas of holy discontent are often the birthplace of vision. It can be painful to dwell on them, but if you are to allow vision to rise, dwell on them you must.

At Limitless, our vision began when we discovered that 111 Elim churches had no young people. It broke our hearts. It was clear to us that unless we helped those churches to change their trajectory, they would die out with their congregations. We had to do something. From our subsequent prayers and discussions the vision was born to 'pioneer 100 new youth ministries through churches who are not currently reaching young people'. We launched a new initiative called Limitless Pioneers, and have since been working with churches all over the nation to start up brand new youth ministries.

Here's the point: our vision was a solution to a problem that we had to do something about.[4]

What are the problems you see that you are compelled to act on? Could it be that God is stirring vision in your heart in that area?

2 Leaders who listen

As you begin to identify the problems that need addressing, it is paramount that we bring them prayerfully before God. Vision is not simply thinking of the next great idea; it's about getting ourselves on God's agenda. That's why God is looking for leaders who are listening. So, have you prayed? Have you fasted? Have you been quiet and waited on God in solitude? Because any vision worth acting on is worth waiting on!

3 Good idea or God idea?

When the Lord begins stirring something in your heart, how do you know if it's really from him? Here are a few checkpoints that might help you.

A God-ordained vision will
- always help fulfil the wider mission of God.
- never contradict Scripture.
- keep you awake at night.
- be too big for you to handle, because divine vision necessitates divine intervention.
- be financially implausible, logistically challenging and practically improbable.
- require a maturity and leadership skill that you don't yet possess, and will thus cause you to place your dependency on God.

From concept to target

As we've said, mission is about *what you do*; vision is about *where you are going*. Thus the key difference between your mission and vision is that your vision must be measurable. Your mission may be more conceptual, setting the general guard rails for your chosen activity, whereas your vision should look more like a target, something very specific you are aiming for. There should be a clear finish line that everyone on the team is seeking to cross.

In *The Four Disciplines of Execution*, Chris McChesney and his team offer a helpful formula for understanding vision: 'X to Y by when'.[5] In other words, a start line, a finish line and a deadline! Every vision should align with this formula because, if your vision is not measurable, how will you know when you have accomplished it?

Having a measurable destination for your team will dramatically increase engagement and accountability, because everyone on the team knows what you are aiming for. This kind of clarity rids the team of ambiguity and engenders a strong sense of shared purpose as you journey together towards a common goal. Communicating your vision as a measurable destination will also ensure your team knows exactly what is important in your children's or youth ministry. It will clearly communicate to everyone involved what your shared priorities are. After all, if we don't measure what we value, we will value what we measure.

What would it look like to move your vision from a *concept* to a *target*? Let's say you want to see the young people in your youth ministry becoming lifelong disciples. Nice concept. But what if you set a target for 50 per cent of your young people to be in discipling relationships with a mature Christian in the next eight months? That's a vision! Or perhaps you've been thinking about putting more focus on outreach to the children in your community. Again, great concept. But how about you set a target to be serving in three primary schools in your city at least once a half-term by the end of the academic year? Now you've got a vision.

Suddenly it becomes a bit more real and a lot more scary! But if we want to see God do something supernatural then we must attempt something that is beyond our natural ability to accomplish. Don't hold back. Dream big. Let vision for transformation stir in your heart. Drive relentlessly towards that vision of a preferred future, and experience the thrill of joining with God's mission to see his kingdom come on earth as in heaven.

Application questions

- What are the things that break your heart or keep you awake at night? Could it be that God is stirring you to do something about it?
- Consider how you could move your vision from a concept to a target. What is your start line (X)? What is your finish line (Y)? And what is your deadline (by when)?

EVERYONE CAN HAVE IDEAS. MOST OF US DESIRE TO DO SOMETHING ABOUT THEM. BUT THE THING THAT MARKS OUT GREAT LEADERS FROM THE REST IS THE ABILITY TO MAKE THOSE IDEAS HAPPEN.

23
MAKING IDEAS HAPPEN

I've had an idea that I reckon is going to make me a fortune around youth and children's ministry conferences: A new line of T-shirts emblazoned with the slogan, 'Administration is not my gift'.

Show me the money!

I jest, of course, but the point is, if you haven't said it yourself you've definitely heard it (or something like it) said by your colleagues in youth and children's ministry. And it's hard to argue. None of us got into youth or children's ministry to complete risk assessments, collate consent forms, manage accounts or fill in registers. These are the necessary evils that accompany the real work of reaching, discipling and investing in the lives of children and young people.

And yet I have a deep concern that there is a leadership essential that we are overlooking, and thus significantly lacking in, because we have incorrectly labelled it 'administration'.

I'm talking about *execution*. Execution and administration are not the same thing. Execution is the difference between having ideas and making ideas happen. It's the difference between dreaming big dreams and living those dreams. Execution is the difference between envisioning change and actually changing things. Not every leader requires a gift of administration, but every leader who wants to be an effective leader must learn the discipline of execution.

In his book *Ego Is the Enemy*, Ryan Holiday writes: 'Our ego wants our ideas, and the fact that we desire to do something about them, to be enough.'[1] But they're not enough. Not nearly enough. Scripture even goes so far as to say, 'it is sin to know what you ought to do and then not do it' (James 4.17, NLT).

Everyone can have ideas. Most of us desire to do something about them. But the thing that marks out great leaders from the rest is the ability to make those ideas happen.

Let's be wary of spending so much time talking about ideas that we convince ourselves we have actually done something about them. Instead, here are six steps you can implement to help take your biggest dreams out of your head and into reality.

1 Begin with the end in mind

Imagine that you jump into your car one morning, pop on your seat belt, turn the key in your ignition, check your mirrors (because you are a highly responsible road user), pull out of your parking space and set off on a journey. But, before too long, panic sets in. Why? Because you have come to a junction and you do not know which way to turn.

OK, OK, I can tell you're not really tracking with my hypothetical road trip, and with good reason: it's never happened to you, and it's never happened to anyone. But that's exactly the point. No one sets out on a journey in their car without a destination in mind, and the fact that they have a predetermined destination ensures that, when they come to a junction, their decision is already made for them. They know where they are going. Their destination determines their direction.

Yet this scenario does play out regularly in our ministries, because we didn't set out on our leadership journey with an end in mind. This means that when we are confronted with a decision, we panic, because we do not know which way to turn.

In order to execute ideas effectively, you need to know where you're going before you set out. Thus, as discussed in the previous chapter, the first step of execution is to have a clearly defined vision.

In *The Seven Habits of Highly Effective People*, Stephen Covey explains:

> To begin with the end in mind means to start with a clear understanding of your destination. It means to know where you're going so that you better understand where you are right now so that the steps you take are always in the right direction.[2]

Which is not to say we will never take a wrong turn (even with the satnav on, we miss a turning every now and then), but it does mean that it won't be long before you realize you're off course. If we don't know where we're going before we set off, we could find ourselves making fast progress along a road that's heading in the wrong direction!

So, what are you aiming for? What's your target? Begin with the end in mind.

2 Most important things first

How do you order your days? Do you get the hardest things out of the way first? Do you warm up gently by getting the easiest things done first? Or perhaps you jump into the most urgent things first?

Unfortunately, none of these will help you effectively execute on ideas. If you wish to arrive at the destination you're aiming for, you must prioritize the things that enable you to get there by giving them the first and best of your time. Don't be tempted to jump straight into your email first thing in the morning. Set aside that time to work on the things that are most important according to your goals, visions and values – which is not the same as the most urgent according to your inbox.

3 Say no to say yes

Once you have a clear idea of what you're aiming for, you have in turn made an advance decision about how you will spend your time – the things you will say yes to and the things you will say no to. Your activity should be determined by vision (predetermined destination), not by demand or even opportunity. But in order to execute ideas effectively you will need to say no to good things in order to protect the time required to deliver on the most important things.

Youth ministry legend Doug Fields explains it like this:

> You need to learn to say no to many good things and wonderful people so you'll have space to say yes to God, yes to the important people in your life, yes to priorities – yes to what matters most.[3]

Don't be afraid to say no to good opportunities, in order to say yes to God opportunities. We'll talk more about this in the next chapter.

4 What, who, when?

Until ideas are rooted in clearly defined action, those ideas will never become reality. Don't move on from that idea until you have clearly defined *what* needs to be done next, *who* is going to do it and, crucially, *when* it needs to get done by. This is even more important when working alone, because no one is keeping you accountable to a deadline. So create a self-imposed deadline and commit to delivering on it.

5 Strategic time for strategic thinking

The number-one enemy to making ideas happen is everyday life. Because new ideas are new, they don't have to be done. For that reason they are the first thing to be forgotten about when life gets busy. This is why you need to carve out some time in your calendar each week to stop and think ahead. Have a pause moment, with your phone off and email shut down, to consider what needs to be done this coming week to execute on your ideas.[4]

6 Block timing

Finally, having considered what needs to get done to make your ideas happen, don't put it on a to-do list. Instead, block out some time in your calendar (or diary) to work on it. That way, when someone asks you for some of your time and you open up your calendar to book it in, the time you need to make your ideas happen doesn't get swallowed up. Plan, prioritize and protect the time you need to execute your dreams.

I appreciate that none of this is particularly sexy, but *dreams don't work if you don't.* When we forgo the leadership skill of execution under the guise of 'administration is not my gift', we are making excuses for our inability to deliver on our ideas. So let's cut this phrase out of our language. We can make excuses or we can make a difference, but we cannot make both.

Application questions

- What are the biggest obstacles in your life that prevent you from executing your ideas? How can you overcome them?
- Of the six steps to making ideas happen, which do you most struggle with and which do you need to implement?

IN ORDER TO SAY YES TO THE GOD THINGS, YOU NEED TO SAY NO TO SOME REALLY GOOD THINGS.

24
DO LESS BETTER

Busy, busy, busy

I'm no prophet, but I do know one thing about you – you are busy! In the whirlwind of youth and children's ministry, you have no problem filling your time. There are innumerable things that you either already are, or feel like you should, be doing: Sunday morning breakout sessions, Friday night outreach groups, small-group Bible studies, mentoring programmes, provision for children with special educational needs, schools ministry, detached work, managing transitions from primary to secondary, preparation for university, writing session content, pastoral conversations, engaging with parents, raising and releasing young leaders, social action projects, recruiting and training volunteers, fund raising, planning events, organizing residentials, sharpening your own gifts, going to training conferences, spending personal time with Jesus, and perhaps even finding a spare moment to read a book like this one! Oh, and then there's those risk assessments to write, DBS checks to process, child protection polices to formulate, finances to reconcile . . . I'm exhausted just thinking about it.

Chances are, you are busting a gut to make all of this happen, and feeling guilty about those things you wish you were doing but can't seem to find the time to give proper attention to. If that's you, I know how you feel. But there is another way.

Do less better

I'm still no prophet, but there's a second thing I know about you: you cannot do everything, and you certainly cannot do everything well. In youth and children's ministry there are so many good things we could be doing, but just because you can do something doesn't necessarily mean you should.

Steve Jobs, the genius behind the rise and rise of Apple, is quoted as saying, 'I'm as proud of what we don't do as I am of what we do.[1] What if the best strategy for you going forward is not to add a new programme but take one way? Not to invest in a new resource but focus on one? Not to launch a new group but shut one down?

Doug Fields makes this salient point:

> When a youth worker is talking about how busy she is, you can be certain something is wrong in her life. Why wrong? God has given us the exact amount of time we need in a given day, week, month and year. If we're too busy, we're not correctly prioritizing our opportunities and managing the time with which God has entrusted us – therefore something must be wrong.[2]

Could it be that you are putting an enormous amount of time, energy and effort into some things you feel you should be doing but have not been called to do? And what if, in order to say yes to the God things, you need to say no to some really good things?

Over the last couple of years I have been asked to be a trustee for the YMCA in a nearby city, invited to sit on the eldership of a local church, and approached to be the chair of trustees of a ministry for which I hold a great deal of admiration. Without doubt, all of these were good opportunities. I felt genuinely privileged to be asked on every occasion, and there were elements of each I would have very much enjoyed. One might even suggest they were positions that could have enhanced my reputation and bumped up my CV. But in the end I said no to all. Why? Because I don't make my decisions on the basis of what they will do for me. And neither should you. Our filter for opportunities is simply to ask, 'What is God calling me to do for him, and will this opportunity enable me to do it?' As kind as it was to have been approached for these opportunities, had I accepted them they would have diverted my time, energy and focus away from God's assignment for my life.

In order to say yes to the God things, you need to say no to some really good things.

The hedgehog concept

In *Good to Great*, Jim Collins writes about the hedgehog concept: in a battle between a fox and a hedgehog, the hedgehog always wins. Why? Because it curls up in a spiky ball so the fox can't eat it. In other words, it does one thing brilliantly. The fox, meanwhile, has all kinds of strategies. He sneaks, he pounces, he attacks from left and right, high and low, but no matter his approach, the hedgehog does the one thing she has mastered and wins every time. In short, 'Hedgehogs see what is essential, and ignore the rest.'[3]

In youth and children's ministry there are so many good things we could be doing, so we strive to do all of them in order to develop a well-rounded ministry. But don't strive to be well rounded; strive to be sharp. Be more hedgehog.

What if we saw what was essential and ignored the rest? How would our ministries change if we learned to do less better? As Andy Stanley writes:

Perhaps the two best kept secrets of leadership are these: 1. The less you do, the more you accomplish. 2. The less you do, the more you enable others to accomplish. By focusing in on only the things that God has specifically called you to do, you free your time, energy, creativity and competency to deliver on those things really well, AND you create opportunities for others to do the things you've stopped doing. Everybody wins![4]

This kind of reductive mindset can feel counter-intuitive but is absolutely liberating. For a start, many of us find our sense of value in busyness: 'If I'm very busy I must be very important.' In addition, we fear stopping things or dropping things because it looks like, and feels like, failure. But what if trying to do everything is actually preventing you from excelling at the main thing? And what if by holding on to all those responsibilities you are robbing somebody else of the opportunities they need to grow? Chances are there are some people around you who are super-passionate about and highly gifted in the things you wish you didn't have to do!

The challenge, then, is to identify and focus on the wildly important and empower the people around you to take a lead on the rest. As Howard Hendricks of Dallas Theological Seminary once said, 'There are many things I can do, but I have to narrow it down to the one thing I must do.'

Good things vs God things

So how do you weed out the *good* activities that are diminishing your capacity to focus on the *God* activities? How do you discover which things you should really go after, give time to and deliver with excellence, and which things (though good) you need to let go?

This bit takes some time. So go and make yourself a brew, grab a notebook and spend some time with Jesus (and then with your team), reflecting on the questions below. Properly considered, these questions have the power to bring to the surface the things that matter most. Once you've discovered them, focus the first and best of your time and energy on them.

You cannot do everything; so rather than attempting to do everything, do less, and do less better.

Application questions

- What are you most deeply passionate about?
- What are you naturally really good at?
- Which one thing would have the biggest impact on your ministry if you could accomplish it in the next six months?
- Which one thing would have the most negative impact on your young people if you stopped doing it?
- If your budget was cut by 50 per cent, which activities would you stop and which would you fight to keep going?
- If your time was cut by 50 per cent, which activities would you continue to do and which would you have to let go?

IF YOU ATTEMPT TO KEEP EVERYONE HAPPY YOU WILL FIND YOURSELF TORN BETWEEN CONFLICTING VIEWS AND SETTLING FOR A MEDIOCRE MIDDLE GROUND WHERE NO ONE GETS OFFENDED BUT FEW ARE IMPACTED.

25

HOW TO LEAD CHANGE

They were impossibly outnumbered. Twenty-four thousand English troops looked up in fear at 60,000 Scots who were better equipped and better positioned to take the day. And yet, this Battle of Flodden did not turn out as anyone had anticipated. As the massive Scottish army began to descend from their higher vantage point towards the seemingly helpless English soldiers, they unexpectedly entered into a marshland and became stuck. Embedded in the ground and unable to move, the English army took full advantage. It is thought that up to 17,000 Scottish soldiers were killed that day. The moral of the story? *They lost because of their inability to move from where they were.*

I wonder if the same could be said of the Church today? Are we losing because we have become stuck? Is our number diminishing because of our inability (or, rather, unwillingness) to change?

Now more than ever the Church is in need of great leadership, because leadership is inherently about change. Tod Bolsinger expresses this perfectly:

leadership is always about personal and corporate transformation. But because we are hard-wired to resist change, every living system requires someone in it to live into and lead the transformation necessary to take us into the future we are resisting. The person who takes responsibility to live into the new future in a transformative way, in relationship to others in the system, is the leader. If someone is not functioning as the leader, the system will always default to the status quo.[1]

The courage to live into and lead transformation is where leadership emerges. It has far less to do with job title or position than a willingness to embrace the pain that comes with challenging the status quo. The way things have always been is subservient to the way things could be, because leadership is about making it better.

Once leaders capture a vision for a preferred future, they cannot let it go. It takes hold of them. They drive relentlessly towards that dream. Their picture of what could happen is enough to give them the courage to stand firm through whatever resistance they must endure to make change happen. This is why change management must be an intrinsic and inseparable part of every leader's toolkit.

But there's a problem: 'we are hard-wired to resist change', because change always requires some discomfort and often necessitates letting go of something that we have become accustomed to and comfortable with. This is why leading change always has been, and always will be, one of the leader's greatest challenges. But we must not shrink back. So how do we lead change effectively?

Don't require certainty

We make a mistake when we wait to be 100 per cent certain before making a decision about change. If we do, we delay for so long that the opportunity passes us by. If you've done your homework, prayed and sought God, and gathered council from wise confidants, you must learn to trust your instincts and make bold decisions without any guarantee that it will work. I am not advocating casting wisdom aside and making rash, reactive decisions here, I'm just saying that no matter how long you wait you are unlikely ever to be more than 80 per cent certain you're making the right change. I don't know about you, but I'd rather give something a go that didn't work out than miss out on an opportunity and always be left wondering what might have happened if I'd had the courage to take a risk.

Exploration before activation

For leadership inspiration and example, the story of Nehemiah is up there with my favourites in all of Scripture. Nehemiah had a vision to rebuild the walls of Jerusalem, but before sharing what was on his heart he took a trip around the walls to see what he was up against. Likewise, when you envision a change, you would be wise to do a bit of exploration before making a decision. Do you know any other youth or kids' workers who have done something similar before, for example? Why not seek them out, ask them questions and visit their ministries? Gathering knowledge and information in this way is not evidence of a lack of faith, but the presence of wisdom. As Jesus himself said, 'Suppose one of you wants to build a tower. Won't you first sit down and estimate the cost to see if you have enough money to complete it?' (Luke 14.28).

Give key stakeholders a voice

Change always goes better when the people it affects the most have been heard. I'm not suggesting you should take a vote; I'm encouraging you to present your ideas to key stakeholders at an early stage and allow them to shape and develop those ideas with you. Crucially, this creates ownership, which vastly increases your chances of taking these people with you when the changes are finally made. So be sure to create spaces to intentionally listen to those who will be affected by the change, and allow their ideas and concerns to influence how you move forward.

Involve your leaders early

Involve your senior leaders early in your thought process when considering significant change. When you speak to them – and this is crucial – ask for their input on your idea; don't just inform them about it. There is a whole world of difference here. You are much more likely to get the go-ahead from your leaders if you take them on the journey rather than inform them of the destination. We'll delve into the principle in greater depth in Chapter 27 on 'How to lead up'.

Communicate why, not just what

When you speak to your key stakeholders, team members, senior leaders or anyone through whom you are trying to lead the change you are envisioning, be sure you don't focus on *what* you want to do, but rather *why* you want to do it. Your why should address two 'locations' – here and there.

First, why can't you stay *here*? Why is it not an option for things to stay as they are right now? Why is it completely essential for change to happen, and why is now the time? Second, why must you go *there*? In what way will the change you are envisioning be a significantly more fruitful and effective option than the way you're doing things right now?

A what without a why is an inconvenience; an apparently unnecessary change for change's sake. But a passionately communicated and compelling why has the power to inspire others to move forward from circumstances they were previously content to live with.

So, be clear about your why, because it's the *why* that gives people a reason to get excited about the *what*.

Don't try to please everyone

You cannot make an omelette without breaking some eggs! Which is to say that no matter how well you follow the aforementioned process, there will always be somebody somewhere who is not happy about the change – but that's OK. If you try to please everyone you'll end up inspiring no one. If you attempt to keep everyone happy you will find yourself torn between conflicting views and settling for a mediocre middle ground where no one gets offended but few are impacted.

Some time ago I caused some significant upset by closing down a number of events, some of which had been running for many years, in order to start something new. This decision was made prayerfully, in consultation with key stakeholders and with robust data to back up our thinking. It was not, however, a decision that we knew would be well received by everyone. Sure enough, I was subject to a few emails and phone calls from people who felt compelled to express their dissatisfaction with my leadership, one of which in particular was very cutting and personal. But the truth is, if we are leading as we should, we will all experience moments like these. That said, the fact that this kind of criticism is an inseparable part of leadership makes it no less easy to receive, especially when it gets personal. So how do we respond? How do we keep our integrity and guard our hearts in these moments?

First, we must work to ensure that our identity is not rooted in the approval or affirmation of people. If we live by compliments we will die by criticism. We must therefore ensure we have a robust personal identity that is rooted in who God says we are, knowing that this does not change with our popularity.

Second, as we discussed in some detail in Chapter 9, 'Thanks for the feedback', we make a choice to listen and to learn, rather than react defensively. Even within that very angry phone call there was a trace of truth to be found, and I managed to learn something that served me well in future change-making.

Third, we ensure we have appropriate avenues through which we can vent our emotions in their most raw and unfiltered form. We do this first with Jesus who offers to carry our burdens. We do this also with trusted confidants who, crucially, are not personally invested in the people or ministries involved. And just in case there was any uncertainty, social media is not the place to vent via ambiguous, passive-aggressive comments about how 'some people are just stuck in the past'. So when you're feeling hurt or angry, stay off your socials!

The honest truth is, if you're not willing for people not to like you every once in a while, then leadership is probably not for you. Look at Jesus. Was he worried about offending people? He was hated because of the changes he was bringing about, but he made them anyway, the legacy of which is that you and I are Christians today. We are the beneficiaries of the criticism he endured to bring about change. Simply put, there is no setting the future without upsetting the present.

As Christian leaders we anchor our practice in the nature of the God we serve; a God who is at once eternally the same (Hebrews 13.8) and making all things new (Revelation 21.5) – and in his likeness we must follow. Our message will remain for ever the same: the gospel is the unchanging truth for all generations. And yet the delivery of that message can and must change from generation to generation.

Leadership and change are two inseparable, and yet sometimes uncomfortable, bedfellows. I pray that in following these steps you will see the changes you've dreamed about become reality, as you courageously go after the future you long to see.

Application questions

- Consider the changes you are seeking to make in your children's or youth ministry. Take a moment to write a list of all the reasons why this change should be made.
- Why can't you stay where you are now? What's at stake?
- What will be better as a result of the changes you are seeking to make?
- Who are the people in your context (senior leaders and key stakeholders who will be affected by the change) whom you need to consult before you start changing things?

DOING CRAZY THINGS BASED ON *GOOD* IDEAS IS NOT GREAT FAITH, IT'S GREAT FOOLISHNESS. DOING CRAZY THINGS BASED ON *GOD* IDEAS IS NOT GREAT FOOLISHNESS, IT'S GREAT FAITH.

26

WISDOM AND RISK: EMBRACING THE TENSION

We all love the story of Simon Peter, right? That memorable moment when – as all of his friends looked on – Peter took a huge risk, stepped out of the boat and began to walk on the water towards Jesus. We love his audacity. We applaud his courage. We're inspired by his faith (even though he sank!). Not only do we all love it, we've all used it in our youth and children's groups. Why? Because this is a story that we are confident will stir the hearts of our children and young people. There's something about the call to adventure that resonates in their spirit. There's something about taking an audacious risk that we know captivates their imagination. Indeed, there's something in every young person that longs to 'step out of the boat'.

How sad it is, then, when age robs us of our audacity. When the passing of years suppresses our 'childlike faith'. But for those of us in leadership, this must not be, for comfort and safety is not the natural habitat of the leader. Leaders thrive in 'out of the boat' territory. They are the first to climb over the edge, step out on the water and say, 'With God the impossible is possible!' As Brennan Manning so eloquently reminds us, 'to live without risk is to risk not living'.[1] That's why I believe it is the call of every leader to continue to be captivated by the Spirit of adventure.

But . . . there's one part of Peter's story we so easily miss. One word that confirms Peter's antics are something to be lauded not laughed at. The hinge upon which Peter's risk should be considered great faith as opposed to great foolishness. The one crucial word upon which this whole story pivots:

'Come,' [Jesus] said.
(Matthew 14.29)

Peter's risk can be considered great faith for one reason alone: he acted in response to the call of his Master. The difference between faith and foolishness is the call of God.

Doing crazy things based on *good* ideas is not great faith, it's great foolishness. Doing crazy things based on *God* ideas is not great foolishness, it's great faith!

I wonder if sometimes in children's and youth ministry we are quick to celebrate risk and slow to commend wisdom. Risk is cool. Risk is sexy. Risk is fun! But wisdom is, well, a bit dull in comparison. It doesn't scan so well in our talks. It doesn't quite capture the imagination in the same way. But without wisdom, risk is foolishness.

All risk and no wisdom leads to empty bank accounts, burnt-out teams and disheartened young people. All wisdom and no risk leads to bored young people, dim faith and plateaued ministries. But when you find that sweet spot between wisdom and risk – wow! That's the place where faith grows, hearts are set on fire and the impossible is made possible.

You lead at your best when embracing the tension between wisdom and risk. When, in response to the voice of God, you make bold moves and take great risks.

So let me propose a question for reflection: if there was a pendulum with risk on one side and wisdom on the other, where would that pendulum land for you? Are you over-cautious? Are you so concerned with handling your responsibilities appropriately that you never do anything that has a high risk of failure? Or are you rash? Never pausing to think before you act? Moving ahead with the latest big idea without pausing to consider if it was actually God's idea?

I pray that you will be both wise and audacious, both shrewd and risky. I pray that you will learn to hear the voice of God, and that when you hear him say 'Come', you will stride courageously into uncharted waters. I pray that you will learn to lead from the sweet spot between wisdom and risk, because incredible things emerge from embracing the tension.

Application questions

- Draw a continuum with 'risky' on one side and 'cautious' on the other. Now put a mark on the continuum that represents you. Are you naturally cautious, or does risk come easy to you?
- Are there big faith steps that you know God is asking you to take but are yet to explore because of the risks involved?
- Is there anything you're attempting that has been motivated more by selfish ambition than by the call of God?

LEADERSHIP IS NOT ABOUT AUTHORITY, IT'S ABOUT INFLUENCE.

27
HOW TO LEAD UP

Like you, I am a person under authority. As a volunteer youth leader at my local church, I report up to our youth pastor, senior pastor and the eldership. Even in my context as National Director of Limitless, I'm not really in charge. I report up to the General Superintendent (that's the boss of the Elim movement) and National Leadership Team. The truth is there are very few of us who are actually in charge.

So perhaps you wanted to start a new initiative, community project or detached team. Maybe you had an idea to bring in a band to do a week of evangelism in your local schools. Whatever it is, there is always someone, somewhere, who can open or close the door to your ideas, and open or close the wallet to fund them. For all our great ideas and hard work, we usually don't make the final decision – we are not *the* leader. That's why, if we want to lead a thriving youth or children's ministry, we must learn to lead up.

When we think about leadership, we usually make the mistake of thinking primarily about the people who are, for want of a better term, 'below' us; the teams and young people we lead and have authority over. But leadership is not about authority, it's about influence. Your job title and job description neither give you influence nor limit it. That's why we need a 360-degree perspective on leadership, where leading those who have authority over us is as important as leading those we have authority over.

So how do we lead the 'gatekeepers' who have the final say? How do we influence those who have authority over us? Be they your vicar, senior pastor, trustees or leadership team, how do we lead up?

Prepare

Before meeting your senior leaders, be that as part of your regular line-management meeting or for a special moment of vision-casting, ensure you are very well prepared. This is about honouring their time. They are probably very busy and don't want to have their time used up with pointless meetings. So, before you go, you should draw up an agenda of things you wish to discuss and send it to them in advance. This will enable them to give some thought to what you want to discuss ahead of time and reduce the risk of having your ideas shut down because of the shock factor! Be careful to think through any questions you might be asked ahead of time and come prepared to answer them, because when you are able to offer quick, accurate answers to their questions you demonstrate competency, which in turn boosts the trust your senior leaders have in you.

Share stories

However, be very careful that your agendas for these meetings don't turn into shopping lists. Our senior leaders will be quickly worn down by constant requests, so make sure you take time in every meeting to share stories of what God is doing among your children and young people. Talk about the child who made a first-time commitment, about the young person who led worship for the first time, and the team member who has stepped up and grown in their own faith because of the opportunity you gave them to lead. This is not about 'blowing your own trumpet' – your senior leaders want to know that God is up to something in your children's and youth ministry. By sharing these stories you will be encouraging them, and as a result they will be more confident to invest in a new idea next time around.

Start with why

We touched on this in Chapter 25 on 'How to lead change', but it's definitely worth revisiting here, because when we have a new idea we so often make the mistake of approaching our senior leaders with only *what* we want to do, when they really need to hear *why* we want to do it.

You want to take your young people on a residential. Why? You want to start up a new youth work on the local estate. Why? You're looking to invest in a new resource for children's church. Why? You're hoping to engage the wider church community in a mentoring programme for your young people. Why? Not just 'what' . . . Why? Because it's the 'why?' that gives them a reason to say 'yes'.

Learning to start with why is to learn the difference between persuasion and inspiration. Great leaders don't only persuade, they inspire. As Simon Sinek says, 'Great leaders are able to create a following of people who act not because they were swayed, but because they were inspired.'[1]

I would therefore argue that until you can answer the following two questions you're not ready to talk to your senior leaders about your new idea:

1 Why do we need to do this?
2 Why does it need to be done now?

The answer to these questions will inspire your senior leaders with the reasons they require to back your vision. Start with why.

Join the dots

You will stand a much better chance of getting the go-ahead if you can join the dots between your vision and the overall vision of the church. If you can frame your ideas within the context of the mission that your senior leaders are seeking to fulfil, if you can describe it using the language of the church mission statement and demonstrate how it will serve to fulfil the 'together' mission your church is pursuing, you are already halfway to the finish line. Perhaps more to the point, your ideas *should* serve the overall vision of the church. Our youth and children's ministries are not isolated silos. While they do have a specific demographic that often requires a different approach, everything we do should be in line with the metanarrative of the whole church community. The first step is to ensure our youth and children's ministries serve the mission and vision of the church; the second is to join the dots for our senior leaders by showing them *how* they are serving it.

Work hard

Now, I know you work hard, I know you give your best, I know you don't spend your days sitting in Starbucks and playing marshmallow towers, but do your senior leaders see that?

I once had a conversation with a senior leader who told me that the main thing their youth worker talked about in his line management meetings was his annual leave. I get that proper rest patterns are important, but that's not good leading up, because it doesn't communicate to your leader that you're hungry, passionate, hard working and determined.

A senior leader wants to know that her youth and children's workers are giving the very best of themselves to further the mission of the team. She wants to see that they are maximizing their time and being faithful stewards of the opportunity they have entrusted to them. It is this kind of self-motivated and diligent youth or children's worker who earns the trust of her senior leaders, making it far more likely she will give them the permission and autonomy they require to pursue that which the Lord is putting on their hearts.

Every leader I know making a significant impact shares a common commitment to hard work. So let's give our best to each day; by doing so we make a difference, we honour God and we honour the leaders who lead us.

Be willing to serve

Leading up is also about a willingness to be led. That means we show a willingness to serve joyfully outside our direct area of responsibility, and an ability to submit when the answer is no.

I am reminded of the words of the author of Hebrews, who encourages us to

> Have confidence in your leaders and submit to their authority, because they keep watch over you as those who must give an account. Do this so that their work will be a joy, not a burden, for that would be of no benefit to you.
> (Hebrews 13.17)

Our senior leaders carry a heavy burden of responsibility, both now and in eternity; they are required to give an account on our behalf! While we are responsible for a specific area of ministry within our churches, they carry the burden for *every* ministry in the Church. It's easy to forget that they are carrying many responsibilities, challenges and conflicts of which we are entirely unaware. So let's do what we can to lighten the load. Let's be youth and children's leaders who are a joy to work with.

Leadership is not about authority, it's about influence. So if God has given us a fresh vision, a new idea or an important responsibility, then let's be good stewards by leading up well.

Application questions

- Do you have a regular meeting with your senior leader? If not, ask for one. I'd suggest once a month as an absolute minimum.
- Take some time to prepare for your next meeting with your senior leader. Which stories of transformed lives will you share? What precisely do you want to discuss? And what information might you send your senior leader in advance to ensure you don't catch him or her off guard?

WE LOSE CONTROL OF OUR TIME BECAUSE WE ARE QUICK TO SAY YES TO OPPORTUNITIES BECAUSE THEY ARE VISIBLE NOT BECAUSE THEY ARE VALUABLE.

28
KILLING TIME?

What would you give for an extra day in your week? How about an extra month in your year? Imagine it! A secret space where you could hide away and complete all of those risk assessments you should have processed but never got around to, plan a year's worth of small-group sessions, get the letters for your residentials together, and maybe even a sneaky holiday. Sounds good, right? Of course it does. Because, like me, you feel under pressure. There are seemingly not enough hours in the day to get everything done. And just when you thought it couldn't get any busier . . . *pastoral crisis alert!* (Which are like buses, right?) So now you're meeting with young people, talking with parents and it knocks you back even further. You haven't seen your friends for two weeks, your personal time with Jesus is out the window, you skipped your day off again. Your only option is to show up to Children's Church and 'wing it' because you ran out of time to get that session planned, and you leave with that dull ache of knowing it could have been better . . . if only you had more time.

Time. There's never enough of it. Right?

Wrong.

According to 2 Peter 1.3, 'His divine power has given us everything we need for a godly life through our knowledge of him who called us by his own glory and goodness' – and *everything* includes time.

It may not feel like it, but God has given you everything you need to be who he is calling you to be. It therefore stands to reason that God's life-giving assignment for you is possible to fulfil in the seven days of the week and 52 weeks of the year he created. So if you feel over-whelmed and out of control, here are three steps you can take to help you get on top of your time.

1 Define your personal mission

In Chapter 21, 'Define your mission', we discussed the primacy of coming to clarity around the mission of your ministry. But what about your personal mission? Who is God calling *you* to be? What is he calling you to do? Answering those questions is the first step in taking back control of your time because, just as with ministry, your mission becomes the filter through which you make decisions about how you will spend this time.

I would encourage you to take thoughtful time in prayer and re-flection to compose a personal mission statement (you can use the exercise at the end of this chapter to help). In doing so you will shed light on the things you are giving your time to that fall outside the things God is asking you to do.

Define your mission. Because where your priorities are, there your time will be.

2 Organize by mission, not opportunity

Once you have defined your mission, the next step is to organize your time around it. Mission, not opportunity, should define your schedule. Instead of asking, 'How can this be done more effec-tively?', ask, 'Does this need to be done at all?' In this way, you begin to filter opportunities according to their relevance to your mission.

Just because we *can* do something doesn't mean we *should*. One of the main reasons we lose control of our time is because we are quick to say yes to opportunities because they are visible not because they are valuable. By defining your mission you create a system through which you can accurately define the value of an opportunity, and thus many of your decisions are already made for you.

For example, it may be that in the process of defining your mission you identify hospitality as a personal value, and as a result become more intentional about opening your home to friends, neighbours, young people and team members. So picture the scene: you're offered a speaking gig at a training conference, having previously arranged for your neighbours to join you for a meal that same evening. The speaking event is an opportunity that is undoubtedly more visible but, according to your personal mission, less valuable. Before going through the process of defining your personal mission you would have either taken the booking and cancelled the meal on the unconsidered premise that the speaking opportunity was of greater value, or tried to rearrange your neighbours to another evening, resulting in another over-scheduled week and a hurried soul. But now that you have clarified your personal mission, the decision is clear; you have chosen to place a high value on hospitality so you politely decline the booking and enjoy a meal with your neighbours. Your time is spent on that which is most valuable and your schedule is not over-burdened. It's a win–win.

If you want to take back control of your time and come alive through living out God's perfect purposes for your life, organize by mission not opportunity.

3 Have the courage to say no

In order to stay mission-centric you'll have to say no to many good opportunities that fall outside the mission you have defined for your life and ministry. If you're anything like me you'll find this is easier said than done. But until you learn to say no to opportunities that fall outside God's remit for your life, you will always feel overwhelmed and out of control. You have to start saying no to good things so that you'll be able to say yes to the best things.

Think for a moment of Jesus. Never has there been a man with a more important God-given assignment. His task was very literally a matter of life or death – for all humankind! Yet, in spite of this, Jesus never seemed overwhelmed or out of control, and he successfully used the short time he had been given to fulfil that assignment. How? Because Jesus had clearly defined his mission, organized his time by mission, and was willing to say no to opportunities that fell outside that mission.

In Luke 4, we read about an occasion when Jesus went back to his home town of Nazareth. On the Sabbath day he visits the synagogue and is handed the scroll of the prophet Isaiah. Jesus could have read anything from that entire book, but he chose to read from what we now know as chapter 61:

'The Spirit of the Lord is on me,
because he has anointed me
to proclaim good news to the poor.
He has sent me to proclaim freedom for the prisoners
and recovery of sight for the blind,
to set the oppressed free,
to proclaim the year of the Lord's favour.'[1]

A verse and a half.

He rolls up the scroll, hands it back to the attendant, and he sits down.

I imagine that all eyes were on him in this moment as the people thought, 'Two verses Jesus, really? Is that all you're gonna read?'

And then he speaks, and he says, 'Today this scripture is fulfilled in your hearing' (Luke 4.21). Mic drop. Exit stage left.

Upon saying that, Jesus made his mission clear. He would align himself with the prisoner, with the poor, with the blind and with the oppressed. Jesus was here for the lost. He declared that day, 'This is what I am here for. This is what I stand for. This is what I live for. This is my *mission*.' Throughout his ministry he would continue to affirm this clarity of purpose with mission statements such as, 'I have not come to call the righteous, but sinners' (Mark 2.17), and, 'the Son of Man came to seek and to save the lost' (Luke 19.10).

But Jesus didn't only have clarity about his mission; he *organized* around his mission. It was his clearly defined purpose, not the demands of the people around him or the next best idea, that guided where he went and when he went there. It was his clearly defined mission that enabled him to say yes, and no, to the opportunities that were presented to him.

Having spent some time ministering in Capernaum, Jesus took some time in solitude to pray, as was his practice. The people came after him asking for more of his time, but Jesus, driven by missional purpose, refuses them:

> At daybreak, Jesus went out to a solitary place. The people were looking for him and when they came to where he was, they tried to keep him from leaving them. But he said, 'I must proclaim the good news of the kingdom of God to the other towns also, because *that is why I was sent.*'
> (Luke 4.42–43)

Such clarity! Such purpose! Such fruitfulness from such a short period of ministry! Truly an example to follow. So how do we get to that place of clarity? How do we discover that same sense of missional purpose that Jesus possessed?

What follows is an adaptation of an exercise published in Stephen Covey's *The Seven Habits of Highly Effective People*[2] to help you write your own personal mission statement. It's an exercise that I have found extremely helpful in my own life. In fact, as I write, I can glance to my left and see my personal mission statement hanging in a frame next to my desk. It continues to be a guiding light for me and I hope it will become the same for you.

Application questions
Writing a personal mission statement

Step 1. Imagine that you're dead (sorry!). If you became everything you are aspiring to be, what would the people closest to you say about you? Write an obituary from the perspective of each of the people below:

- spouse
- firstborn child
- best friend
- neighbour
- someone who served under your leadership.

Remember, the key is to be aspirational; to write what they might say if you actually became everything you wanted to be, rather than what they might write if you died now! And please note, you don't have to be presently married, or a parent, and so on, to fulfil the exercise. The question is, *if* you were married and died, what might your spouse say about you? Got it? OK, go . . .

Step 2. Now write a list of values based on those obituaries. For example, if you've written, 'I could always count on them to listen when I needed help,' then one of your values might be 'good listener'. If you've written, 'I always felt better for having spent time with them,' one of your values might be 'inspiring'. At this stage you are simply aiming to draw out a list of the values that are important to you.

Step 3. Finally, draft a personal mission statement based on your list of values. This could be in the form of bullet points, paragraphs or even a poem. Just be creative and write in a way that feels natural to you. I include my own personal mission statement below as an example, not to imitate but to give a tangible idea of how you might go about creating yours.

My personal mission statement – an example

- I will love God by serving him when I feel like it and when I don't.
- I will give my life to helping those who are far from God discover full life through Jesus.
- I will make personal sacrifices to demonstrate love to my family.
- I will model in my life the things I want to see developed in those I lead and love.
- I will choose to look at every person and situation with an unevenly positive perspective, and ruthlessly eliminate cynicism from my life.
- I will be consistent and even-tempered through the inconsistent and uneven circumstances of life.

- I will be unswerving in my commitment to those people and ministries to which God has called me.
- I will honour God by deliberately and strategically nurturing and multiplying the gifts, strengths and opportunities with which he has entrusted me.
- I will actively humble myself, putting to death the poisons of selfish ambition with the help of his Holy Spirit.
- I will seek to be sensitive to the whispers of the Holy Spirit, ready and willing to take risks and make sacrifices in order to boldly and passionately follow my Lord.
- I will not take myself too seriously and be sure to laugh a lot.

Now it's your turn!

OUR VIEW OF EXCELLENCE HAS BECOME TOO NARROW. WE HAVE CONFUSED EXCELLENCE WITH PRODUCTION VALUE.

29

EXCELLENCE IS NOT A SWEAR WORD

All leaders should strive for excellence in their ministry.

There, I said it.

For some readers, that is a non-statement. To them, the pursuit of excellence is a prerequisite for every servant of Christ. They associate excellence with worship, seeking to give their best offering to God in all they do.

There are others, however, who have not made it to this paragraph because they have already thrown this book at the wall! For these readers, excellence is exclusive, resulting in a professionalized Church where only the elite are allowed to participate, while the more ordinary among us sit at the sidelines and watch on, as though attending a concert rather than participating in authentic community. And with these readers I hold some sympathy. Too often we profess a theology of the priesthood of all believers – where 'to each one the manifestation of the Spirit is given for the common good' (1 Corinthians 12.7), and where 'Each of you should use whatever gift you have received to serve others' (1 Peter 4.10) – while in practice only the gifts of the teaching pastor and a few talented musicians are expressed. The pursuit of excellence does indeed go wrong when it causes our practice to subvert our theology, shutting down the opportunity for the 'priesthood' (that's everyone) to use their gifts in the service of God and his Church.

Our view of excellence has become too narrow. We have confused excellence with production value, as though excellence in the kingdom of God equates to bright lights and smoke machines. And while the creativity that goes into a well-designed stage can indeed be part of our worship (we need only look at the detailed instructions for building the tabernacle in the closing chapters of Exodus to see that environment matters to God), excellence in the kingdom is far more expansive than the things we usually associate with the gathered Church. Kingdom-excellence extends to excelling in character, in relationships, in disciple-making, in creativity, in hospitality, in artistry, and in love. It's about flourishing in the gifts the Lord has given us, and creating opportunities for others to do the same.

I therefore dare to suggest that excellence and opportunity are not mutually exclusive and, for that reason, excellence is not a swear word.

Why excellence matters

1 Excellence honours God

I am fortunate enough to live in the beautiful town of Malvern. A brisk 20-minute walk from my office door takes me to the top of the Worcestershire Beacon, the tallest of the Malvern hills. From there, in daylight hours, I can see for miles around. At night, far away from the city lights, I can see stars without number blanketing the sky. On both occasions it is clear to me that our God is a God of excellence! In creativity? Excellent. In beauty? Excellent. In diversity? Excellent. In grandeur? Excellent! When God created a home for us, he did it with the utmost excellence. Should that which we offer in service and worship of him be any less? Indeed not.

When the Lord gave instructions to Moses about how God's people should worship him, he decreed that only an offering without 'defect' would be accepted (Leviticus 22.20). Later on, the Lord rebuked his people for failing to offer the very best of their flock (Malachi 1.6–14). And most importantly, as Pastor Perry Noble reminds us:

> When it came to redeeming mankind, Jesus did not search the back corners of heaven to find some under-challenged angel who had nothing to do . . . he came, he did it, he paid for the sin of the world! He gave his best, and his followers should do the same.[1]

We are to give God our best, because he gave his best to us. I love how Shelley Giglio, co-founder of the Passion Movement, implores us to pursue excellence on this basis, saying:

> God is an excellent God. He does things as well as possible. So should we. We want to do things the best we can do it, because God deserves our very best. God living in us informs the way we do things and the kind of excellence that God demands.[2]

Excellence honours God.

2 Excellence inspires people

We see this principle at work in Scripture in the life of Daniel. Daniel 6.3 (ESV) tells us that 'Daniel became distinguished above all the other high officials and satraps'. Why? 'Because an excellent spirit was in him.' And what happened as a result? 'The king gave thought to setting him over the whole realm.' It was Daniel's pursuit of excellence that paved the way for him to have a significant kingdom impact in a pagan nation.

One concern often raised when the language of 'excellence' is used in church circles is about the danger of creating an exclusive environment, where only the most talented are allowed to participate. And while that can be the outcome of excellence perverted, I would argue that a lack of excellence has the potential to exclude in equal measure.

Imagine a youth ministry where the environment is cold, the decor dated, the music irrelevant, the band insensitive and the communication boring. In this kind of setting, the long-standing Christian young person may continue to engage week after week because of two pre-existing relationships: first, her relationship with God, through which she finds meaning in the experience; second, her relationships with the people involved in the gathering. Her pre-existing relationships cause her to return *in spite of* the quality of the experience.

Now imagine a new young person showing up to that environment. He has no pre-existing relationships to return for, and this is his first encounter with church of any kind. The environment is dated, the songs unrecognizable, the music bad, and he is bored by the communication. Is he coming back next week? No chance! So you see, because of the lack of excellence, insiders are included, while outsiders are excluded. Tim Keller makes this case perfectly:

> The quality of the music, your speech, and even the visual aesthetics in worship will have a marked impact on evangelistic power . . . In many churches, the quality of the music is mediocre or poor, but it does not disturb the faithful. Why? Their faith makes the words of the song meaningful, despite its lack of artistic expression; what's more, they usually have a personal relationship with the music presenter. But any outsider who comes in as someone unconvinced of the truth and

having no relationship to the presenter will likely be bored or irritated by the expression. In other words, *excellent aesthetics includes outsiders, while mediocre aesthetics excludes.* The low level of artistic quality in many churches guarantees that only insiders will continue to come.[3]

Thus, excellence does not have to equate to exclusive.

To be clear, this is not a call to perfection, it's a call to bring our best offering to God; to do the very best with what we have in our hands. God gave us his very best, so we will give him ours.

Make excellence a non-negotiable in your ministry. To paraphrase the great Walt Disney, do what you do so well that your children and young people will want to come back next week and bring their friends.

Excellence is not a swear word.

Application questions

- Consider some examples of excellent children's or youth ministry that you have experienced. What was it that made them excellent?
- Take a moment to review the various areas of your children's or youth ministry. Could they be described as excellent? If not, how can you make adjustments to ensure they are the best they can possibly be with the resources you have available to you?

OUR INABILITY TO RESPOND TO THE MOVE OF THE SPIRIT IS OFTEN LINKED TO BEING OVERLY INVESTED IN OUR METHODS, EVENTS, RESOURCES AND PROGRAMMES, SO THAT IT BECOMES HARD TO LAY THEM DOWN WHEN GOD CALLS US FORWARD.

30

KEEPING IN STEP WITH THE SPIRIT

If I were to invite you to my home there would be a number of ways I could help you get there. The easiest way would be to give you my postcode to pop into your satnav. The throwback approach would be to give you a map with a step-by-step guide from where you are now to where you are going. The other method would be to get in the car in front of you and say, 'Follow me.' To reach your destination in this way you would have to drive at my speed, be alert to my signals, take my turnings and follow my lead. In short, you would have to keep your eyes on me.

This is the way the Lord leads us. He doesn't give us a step-by-step plan, outlining every direction upfront, as much as we might like him to! Instead he goes before us and says, 'Follow me.' Why? Because it causes us to keep our eyes on him. It draws us into a moment-by-moment dependence upon him. It requires that we follow his lead. It demands that we 'keep in step with the Spirit' (Galatians 5.25).

We see this in Scripture when the Lord led the people of Israel through the wilderness via a pillar of cloud in the day and fire at night. Their path was not set out in full; they were required to move step by step, moment by moment, in response to the movements of God.

> Whenever the cloud lifted from above the tent, the Israelites set out; wherever the cloud settled, the Israelites set up camp. At the LORD's command the Israelites set out, and at his command they set up

camp. As long as the cloud stayed over the tabernacle, they remained in camp. When the cloud remained over the tabernacle a long time, the Israelites obeyed the LORD's order and did not set out. Sometimes the cloud was over the tabernacle for only a few days; at the LORD's command they would set up camp, and then at his command they would set out.
(Numbers 9.17–20)

The people of Israel justifiably get a lot of stick for their often questionable behaviour during their time in the desert, but here's one thing I reckon they did get right: they postured themselves to be ready for change. They were attentive enough to be alert to the movements of God and agile enough to respond quickly.

Could the same be said of your leadership, I wonder? Are you sensitive enough to know when God is moving and courageous enough to follow when he does?

If you find this difficult, it could be because one or more of the following obstacles to keeping in step with the Spirit are present in your life.

1 Married to methods

The reason the people of Israel were able to quickly respond to the movement of God was because they lived in tents, not buildings. Thus, when the cloud moved they could quickly pack everything down, move to a new location, and set it up again in a different configuration. Our inability to respond to the move of the Spirit is often linked to being overly invested in our methods, events, resources and programmes, so that it becomes hard to lay them down when God calls us forward. If we want to be leaders who keep in step with the Spirit, we must learn to see our activity and methodology as tents not buildings, so that we can be flexible enough to move on from them quickly when the Lord is doing a new thing.

2 Busyness

Youth and children's ministry is busy. That's good! We are about the work of the kingdom. But there is such a thing as *too busy*. You know you're too busy when you don't have enough time to stop, reflect and pray about what you're doing. Your eyes are so fixed on the work that's happening 'on the ground' that you don't have time to look up to see if the cloud has moved. The danger here is that you continue to do things that were once of God but that he has long since moved on from, which you failed to notice because you were too busy to stop, look up, think big picture and consider where the Lord was moving next.

3 Fear of failure

It is difficult to keep in step with the Spirit when we are afraid of getting it wrong. This fear can be rooted in pride (we don't want to damage our personal reputation) or over-cautiousness (we want to have all the questions answered and uncertainties removed before moving forward). Either way, keeping in step with the Spirit requires the courage to follow his lead into the unknown, with no guarantees that it will work out. This requires courage and trust in God.

4 Imitating others

There's a fine line between inspiration and imitation. It's good to be inspired by leaders and ministries that are doing great things for the Lord, but we run into trouble when we think that imitating their methods is the key to success. It's not. The key to success is keeping in step with the Spirit. What if the Lord is asking you to do something entirely different from that humongous youth or children's ministry down the road, but you missed it because you were trying to make your ministry more like theirs? It's good to learn and grow through others, but not at the expense of leaning into the unique calling and purpose God has over your life, and following hard after that.

5 Unwillingness to offend people

The challenge we must face when seeking to keep in step with the Spirit is that the people we are leading often like it where we are camping right now! Any movement will always upset someone, no matter how sensitively you navigate the transition. So, yes, we should lovingly try to take everyone with us, but we should not allow our reluctance to upset people to stop us from following after the cloud.

I once heard apologist Amy Orr-Ewing say, 'Whenever God's people endeavour to do God's work it will not go unopposed . . . You have not really led until you have been opposed.' In other words, you cannot keep everyone happy *and* do what God is calling you to do. Why is this true? Because leadership is not about maintenance, it's about movement. So, do we patiently, gently and graciously engage with people's concerns and questions? Absolutely. But do we try to please everyone? Absolutely not – because pleasing people must never become more important than obeying God. After all, I'd rather follow God with a small band of adventurers than with a comfortable crowd.

Since we live by the Spirit, let us keep in step with the Spirit. Look up, follow the cloud and go where the Lord is leading you today.

Application questions

- Of the five obstacles discussed in this chapter, which is the most likely to prevent you from keeping in step with the Spirit?
- What safeguards do you need to put in place to ensure these obstacles do not stop you from obediently pursuing God?
- Is there anything in your youth or children's ministry that the Lord was once in but has since moved on from? Is it time to retire or renew these initiatives?
- When was the last time you stopped to look up and see if 'the cloud' had moved on? Do you need to schedule some time in your calendar for some big-picture thinking and strategic planning?

DURING YOUR LIFETIME YOU MAY WELL DO SOMETHING OTHER THAN YOUTH OR CHILDREN'S MINISTRY. YOU WILL NEVER DO SOMETHING MORE IMPORTANT.

AFTERWORD
YOU WILL NEVER GET A PROMOTION

> Small things are indeed small, but faithfulness in small things is a great thing.
> Mother Teresa

In the process of writing this book I was asked, 'Why don't you just write this for *all* leaders? Surely the principles are transferable.' And yes, indeed they are. The principles discussed in this book will serve you well in any arena of leadership in which you find yourself. With a few quick tweaks to the language, illustrations and application questions, this could easily have been a general leadership book, which in turn would have been made available to a wider audience. But with *Leadership 101* being my first book, there was no doubt in my mind about who I was writing it for. I was writing it for my heroes – the youth and children's leaders who have dedicated their lives to passing on the gospel to the next generation.

Let me repeat what I said earlier: youth and children's ministry is too often seen as a 'stepping stone' into adult ministry, or a 'training ground' in which people can learn until they 'step up' into the 'real thing'. This has led to a damaging, transient culture in youth and children's ministry where we seldom stay in our posts for longer than a few years. There are a number of problems associated with this short-termism. First, it's very difficult to build something significant in such a short period of time.

Second, just when our children and young people are beginning to trust us, we move on, another leader takes our place, and our children and young people have to start all over again. And, third, we have too few seasoned experts in youth and children's ministry, because expertise cannot be built in a few years; it usually takes decades of reflective practice to master something.

So we have a problem. Sometimes we move on because the narrative of the Church is that youth and children's ministries are the places we go to learn our trade before we can be trusted to take a 'step up' on our ministry journey. Believing this, we take on another ministry role because it looks like 'promotion'. At other times we move on because our pay structures don't allow us to stay the course for many decades. We get married, have children and, somewhat ironically, children's and youth ministry becomes no longer financially viable. And I get that. It's hard.

Either way, I'm using the final pages of this book to honour those of you who have stayed the course, and to encourage those of you who are beginning your journey in youth and children's ministry to do the same.

During your lifetime you may well do something other than youth or children's ministry. You could do something that is more public or impressive. You could do something that is held in higher esteem by the watching world. You could surely do something that pays you more, or has a better career path. But please hear me now: *you will never do something more important.*

Seriously, think about it. What could possibly be more important than passing on the gospel to the next generation? I cannot think of a single thing! In that way, you *cannot* get a promotion; there is no higher level!

And, yes, sometimes it's a grind; it's occasionally monotonous and often very painful. But please know this: you are literally changing the future. When you meet that young person for a one-to-one, you are changing the future. When you open the Bible together and the light goes on, you are changing the future. When that young person breaks through from self-harm, you are changing the future. When a child gives their life to Jesus for the first time, you are changing the future. And in countless other ways that you will never perceive this side of eternity, you are changing the future.

So, my dear friend and colleague, thank you. Thank you for all your energy, your effort, your passion, your persistence, your sacrifice. You may not always be seen or thanked, but your name resounds in heaven!

I simply cannot conceive of anything more important that you could give your life to than passing on the gospel to the next generation. So, please, keep doing it, don't give up. The smile of God is over your life today.

You are serving Jesus.

You are making a difference.

You are changing lives.

You are raising a generation.

And you will never get a promotion.

NOTES

Preface: Rise and fall

1 J. C. Maxwell, *The 21 Indispensable Qualities of a Leader* (Nashville, TN: Thomas Nelson, 1999), p. xi.

Introduction: Sharpen the saw

1 S. Covey, *The Seven Habits of Highly Effective People* (London: Simon & Schuster, 1989), p. 51.

1 The ten most important things a leader should do every week

1 H. Nouwen, *Making All Things New* (New York: HarperCollins, 1981), p. 71.

2 B. Lomenick, *The Catalyst Leader: 8 Essentials for Becoming a Change Maker* (Nashville, TN: Thomas Nelson, 2013), p. 185.

3 This is a favourite saying of Pastor Duncan Clark, senior leader of Coventry Elim Church.

4 <https://globalleadership.org/articles/leading-yourself/jo-saxton-level-up-your-leadership/>.

5 R. Bell, *Velvet Elvis: Repainting the Christian Faith* (Grand Rapids, MI: Zondervan, 2006), p. 117.

2 Pause, reflect, innovate, repeat

1 P. Scazzero, *The Emotionally Healthy Leader* (Grand Rapids, MI: Zondervan, 2015), p. 38.

3 Model it

1 D. Kinnaman, *You Lost Me: Why Young Christians Are Leaving*

Church . . . and Rethinking Faith (Grand Rapids, MI: Baker Books, 2011), p. 232.

4 Choose your attitude

1 S. Covey, *The Seven Habits of Highly Effective People* (London: Simon & Schuster, 1989), p. 71.

5 Discover your passion

1 <https://biblehub.com/greek/2204.htm>.
2 B. Lomenick, *The Catalyst Leader: 8 Essentials for Becoming a Change Maker* (Nashville, TN: Thomas Nelson, 2013), pp. 55–6.
3 J. Collins, *Good to Great: Why Some Companies Make the Leap . . . and Others Don't* (London: Random House Business, 2001), p. 109.

6 Passion killers

1 As quoted in M. Summerfield, *Don't Make History Change the Future* (Luton: Urban Saints, 2012), pp. 58–9.
2 B. Manning, *The Signature of Jesus: Living a Life of Holy Passion and Unreasonable Faith* (Colorado Springs, CO: Multnomah, 1988), pp. 103–4.
3 <https://globalleadership.org/search/lived%20with%20passionate%20clarity>.
4 M. Batterson, *Chase the Lion* (Colorado Springs, CO: Multnomah, 2016), p. 170.
5 As quoted in C. Gallo, *Talk Like TED* (New York: St Martin's Press, 2014), p. 37.

7 Humble leaders are better leaders

1 J. Collins, *Good to Great: Why Some Companies Make the Leap . . . and Others Don't* (London: Random House Business, 2001), pp. 12–13, 21.
2 P. Lencioni, *The Five Dysfunctions of a Team: A Leadership Fable* (San Francisco, CA: Jossey-Bass, 2002).

10 The new rules of social media

1 Youth for Christ, *Gen Z: Rethinking Culture* (Halesowen: Youth for Christ, 2017).

2 <www.wired.co.uk/article/uk-spends-more-time-online-sleeping>.

3 <www.businessinsider.com/dscout-research-people-touch-cell-phones-2617-times-a-day-2016-7?r=US&IR=T>.

4 <www.axios.com/sean-parker-unloads-on-facebook-god-only-knows-what-its-doing-to-our-childrens-brains-1513306792-f855e7b4-4e99-4d60-8d51-2775559c2671.html>.

5 Sparks and Honey Culture Forecast, 'Gen Z 2025: The Final Generation', p. 25. See <www.sparkandhoney.com/gen-z>.

6 <www.theatlantic.com/magazine/archive/2017/09/has-the-smartphone-destroyed-a-generation/534198/>.

7 <www.sciencedirect.com/science/article/pii/S0747563216307543?via%3Dihub>.

Introduction: 'A genius with a thousand helpers'

1 As quoted in J. Dickson, *Humilitas: A Lost Key to Life, Love, and Leadership* (Grand Rapids, MI: Zondervan, 2011), p. 36.

2 J. Collins, *Good to Great: Why Some Companies Make the Leap . . . and Others Don't* (London: Random House Business, 2001), p. 45.

3 M. Breen, *Multiplying Missional Leaders* (Pawleys Island, SC: 3DM International, 2012), p. 4.

11 Culture club

1 P. Scazzero, *The Emotionally Healthy Leader* (Grand Rapids, MI: Zondervan, 2015), p. 213.

2 As quoted in T. Bolsinger, *Canoeing the Mountains: Christian Leadership in Uncharted Territory* (Downers Grove, IL: InterVarsity Press, 2015), p. 73.

3 L. Wiseman, *Multipliers: How the Best Leaders Make Everyone Smart* (New York: HarperCollins, 2017), p. 264. Wiseman's quotations are taken from <www.Merriam-Webster.com>.

4 Bolsinger, *Canoeing the Mountains*, p. 73.

5 H. Cloud, *Boundaries for Leaders: Results, Relationships, and Being Ridiculously in Charge* (New York: HarperCollins, 2013).

6 M. Breen, *Multiplying Missional Leaders* (Pawleys Island, SC: 3DM International, 2012), p. 111.

7 P. Lencioni, *The Advantage: Why Organizational Health Trumps Everything Else in Business* (San Francisco, CA: Jossey-Bass, 2012), p. 91.

8 For more on this, see Chapter 14, 'Shoot the elephant'.

9 Wiseman, *Multipliers*, p. 274.

10 A. Stanley, *Making Vision Stick* (Grand Rapids, MI: Zondervan, 2007), pp. 40–1.

12 The value of values

1 P. Lencioni, *The Advantage: Why Organizational Health Trumps Everything Else in Business* (San Francisco, CA: Jossey-Bass, 2012), p. 95.

2 Lencioni, *The Advantage*, p. 98.

3 Lencioni, *The Advantage*, p. 97.

4 Lencioni, *The Advantage*, pp. 93–4.

5 If you'd like to take your team through this exercise, I'd highly recommend picking up a copy of Lencioni's *The Advantage*, which can take you into much greater detail than the format of our discussion permits us to delve into here.

13 Creating community

1 T. Bolsinger, *Canoeing the Mountains: Christian Leadership in Uncharted Territory* (Downers Grove, IL: InterVarsity Press, 2015), p. 156.

16 Building diverse leadership teams

1 B. Lindsay, *We Need to Talk about Race: Understanding the Black*

Experience in White Majority Churches (London: SPCK, 2019),
pp. 98–9.

2 B. Brown, *Dare to Lead: Brave Work. Tough Conversations. Whole Hearts* (Ebury Publishing, 2018).

17 Pay it forward: raising leaders

1 D. Strickland at < https://globalleadership.org/grow/growthtracks/
danielle-strickland-empowerment-women-men-2/>.

2 M. Breen, *Multiplying Missional Leaders* (Pawleys Island, SC: 3DM
International, 2012), p. 68.

3 See Chapter 14, 'Shoot the elephant', and Chapter 19, 'Thanks for
the feedback', for more on this.

19 Thanks for the feedback

1 Shout out to Matt Summerfield for dropping this bit of wisdom.

20 How not to hate meetings

1 S. Sinek, *Start with Why: How Great Leaders Inspire Everyone to
Take Action* (London: Penguin, 2009), p. 99.

21 Define your mission

1 T. Bolsinger, *Canoeing the Mountains: Christian Leadership in
Uncharted Territory* (Downers Grove, IL: InterVarsity Press, 2015),
p. 125.

2 Bolsinger, *Canoeing the Mountains*, p. 128.

22 Vision: from concept to target

1 A. Stanley, *Visioneering: God's Blueprint for Developing and
Maintaining Vision* (Colorado Springs, CO: Multomah Books,
1999), p. 18.

2 < https://globalleadership.org/articles/leading-organizations/aja-
brown-when-vision-overcomes/>.

3 Stanley, *Visioneering*, p. 17.

4 A paraphrase from Andy Stanley's excellent book on vision, *Visioneering*. 'A vision is a solution to a problem that has to be resolved immediately.'

5 C. McChesney, S. Covey and J. Huling, *The Four Disciplines of Execution* (London: Simon and Schuster, 1989), p. 37.

23 Making ideas happen

1 R. Holiday, *Ego Is the Enemy: The Fight to Master Our Greatest Opponent* (London: Profile Books, 2016).

2 S. Covey, *The Seven Habits of Highly Effective People* (London: Simon and Schuster, 1989), p. 98.

3 D. Fields, *What Matters Most: When No Is Better than Yes* (Grand Rapids, MI: Zondervan, 2006), p. 21.

4 For more on this, see Chapter 2, 'Pause, reflect, innovate, repeat'.

24 Do less better

1 As quoted in Steve Jobs, 'Magic Kingdom', *Bloomberg Businessweek*, 6 February 2006.

2 D. Fields, *What Matters Most* (Grand Rapids, MI: Zondervan, 2006), p. 78.

3 J. Collins, *Good to Great: Why Some Companies Make the Leap . . . and Others Don't* (London: Random House Business, 2001), p. 91.

4 A. Stanley, *Next Generation Leader: Five Essentials for Those who Will Shape the Future* (New York: Random House, 2003), p. 17.

25 How to lead change

1 T. Bolsinger, *Canoeing the Mountains: Christian Leadership in Uncharted Territory* (Downers Grove, IL: InterVarsity Press, 2015), p. 21.

26 Wisdom and risk: embracing the tension

1 B. Manning, *The Signature of Jesus: Living a Life of Holy Passion and Unreasonable Faith* (Colorado Springs, CO: Multnomah, 1988), p. 174.

27 How to lead up

1 S. Sinek, *Start with Why: How Great Leaders Inspire Everyone to Take Action* (London: Penguin, 2009), p. 6.

28 Killing time?

1 Isaiah 61.1–2a, as quoted by Jesus in Luke 4.18–19.
2 S. Covey, *The Seven Habits of Highly Effective People* (London: Simon and Schuster, 1989).

29 Excellence is not a swear word

1 P. Noble, 'Four Problems the Church Has Got to Deal With!', 19 April 2012; <https://perrynoble.com/blog/four-problems-the-church-has-got-to-deal-with>.
2 S. Giglio, as quoted in B. Lomenick, *The Catalyst Leader: 8 Essentials for Becoming a Change Maker* (Nashville, TN: Thomas Nelson, 2013), p. 77.
3 T. Keller, *Center Church: Doing Balanced, Gospel-Centered Ministry in Your City* (Grand Rapids, MI: Zondervan, 2012). Emphasis added.